# OUTSTANDING LESSON AHEAD

A guide to creativity, engagement and motivation in the classroom.

AMY SARGENT

JNPAQUET Books Ltd
— LONDON —

**Published by JNPAQUET Books Ltd, LONDON.**

Copyright © 2014 JNPAQUET Books Ltd.
Copyright © 2014 Amy Sargent.

All rights reserved.

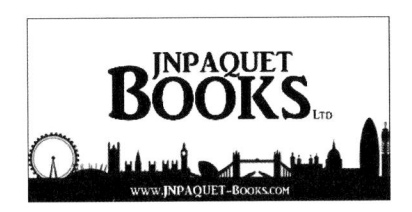

PRINTED IN DECEMBER 2014 IN THE UNITED STATES OF AMERICA.

Copyright © 2014 by Amy Sargent. Illustrations, photographs & text copyright.

The right of Amy Sargent to be identified as the Author of the Work has been asserted by her in accordance with the Copyright, Designs and Patent Act 1988. All rights reserved. No part of this publication may be reproduced, stored in a retrieval system, or transmitted, in any form or by any means without the prior written permission of the author, nor be otherwise circulated in any form of binding or cover other than that in which it is published and without a similar condition being imposed on the subsequent purchaser. To publish, republish, copy or distribute this book, please contact: contact@jnpaquet-books.com

Some illustrations used in this book were designed by Freepik.com

"Outstanding Lesson Ahead" illustrations, photographs, names and related indicia are © 2014, Amy Sargent - All rights reserved.

First Edition Copyright © 2014, JNPAQUET Books Ltd. All rights reserved.
A CIP catalogue record for this title is available from the British Library.

ISBN 9781505543384 (PAPERBACK)
eISBN 9782365212502 (EBOOK)

# CONTENTS

|     | INTRODUCTION |     |
| --- | --- | --- |
| 1.  | ESTABLISH A ROUTINE | 3 |
| 2.  | KEY QUESTIONS | 5 |
| 3.  | STARTERS | 7 |
| 4.  | DIFFERENTIATION | 13 |
| 5.  | AFL TECHNIQUES | 19 |
| 6.  | QUESTIONING | 33 |
| 7.  | MARKING/RESPONDING TO MARKING | 41 |
| 8.  | INCORPORATING LITERACY AND NUMERACY | 55 |
| 9.  | SHOWING PROGRESS / PROGRESS OVER TIME | 60 |
| 10. | CO-OPERATIVE LEARNING/ACTIVE LEARNING | 72 |
| 11. | BEHAVIOUR MANAGEMENT | 84 |
| 12. | PRAISE AND REWARDS | 88 |
| 13. | LEARNING ENVIRONMENT | 94 |
| 14. | USE OF THE TEACHING ASSISTANT | 100 |
| 15. | GAMES | 106 |
| 16. | ENDING THE LESSON — PLENARY TIME | 116 |
|     | DEDICATION | 127 |

# INTRODUCTION

So, why did I write this book? It started with me just wanting to do it for myself so that I did not forget any ideas, but as I added more and more strategies, I thought it would be a useful guide to share with other teachers because teachers are like magpies, always looking for something new and shiny, right? For me, finding a new teaching idea is like Christmas Day. I get excited about how I can use it, how it will link to the current topic and how the kids will respond to it. In fact, I will often be in Tesco trying to think of what dinner I can have, which won't take too much time and effort because I've got a pile of books to mark, but I will end up being sidetracked by some teddy bear shaped post-it notes or inflatable crowns (you have to read the whole book to find out more about this!). I cannot even go to the 99p shop without buying something that I adapt to a prize or game. The place is like teaching idea heaven! Ultimately, my thoughts when compiling my ideas is that, if we urge our students to think, pair and share, why not us too?

The aim of this book is to provide fresh, adaptable ideas without having to trawl through unwanted and unnecessary content. I have purchased many teaching books in the past. During my teacher-training year, I thought it would be a great idea to buy EVERY recommended book on the reading list. Needless to say, I am still skint (some of them were super expensive!) and I am still working my way through them now. Although I have gained ideas from many of the books, they were not always straightforward to find, and many did not apply to my subject. In reality, most teachers who buy teaching guides already know the basics of what AfL is, you also know the importance of differentiation, and you understand the need for praise. What you are really looking for, especially if you are anything like me, is an inspiration; an idea to steal or adapt.

So, having said that, I hope that it is what this book does. I hope it helps you incorporate some strategies in your lessons, which lead them to be outstanding. I have aimed to include generic strategies that are suitable for any level of teacher, any year group and any subject, because there is nothing worse than buying a book and finding that all the strategies are only really suited to one particular subject.

Some of the ideas will require you to open your imagination in order to use them, but I sincerely hope that, by the time you get to the end of the book, you will have found ideas that you are excited about and that you will want to put in place first thing tomorrow morning with bottom set Year 8, because quite frankly you have tried everything with little Joe who cannot sit down and sings every word he says, and you desperately need a new form of behaviour management!

Ultimately, I am passionate about what I do, and I hope that comes across in this book.

**Amy Sargent,**
**13 November 2014.**

# 1. ESTABLISH A ROUTINE

**Consistency is the key to helping pupils progress.**

Consider yourself a trainer, not just a teacher! Whilst it is possible to pull an outstanding lesson "out of the bag" the most outstanding teachers are those who set routines and stick by them. That is not to say that every lesson is the same but more so that the main features of their lessons such as progress checks, questioning, rewards, etc., are all consistent and students know what to expect.

Lay the board out the same for each and every lesson where possible. Students should eventually know to come in and write the date and title (if necessary) and they should have something (settler/starter/thunk) to be getting on with, without you even having to ask. Create a routine whereby colours mean something. For example, anything blue means you must copy, anything red means you must do and anything green is a challenge.

Give students a clear time limit on when you expect things to be done by. This could be signalled by the end of a song/buzzer, etc.

Greet students at the door and where possible have books and resources out ready. If not, provide the students with roles such as book manager, equipment organiser and rewards manager.

## Good to Outstanding

Date: Thursday 16th October

1: Using the legs of Barry the spider, can you think of 8 strands which make up a _GOOD_ lesson?

Extension: Can you find one word for each letter of the word OUTSTANDING?

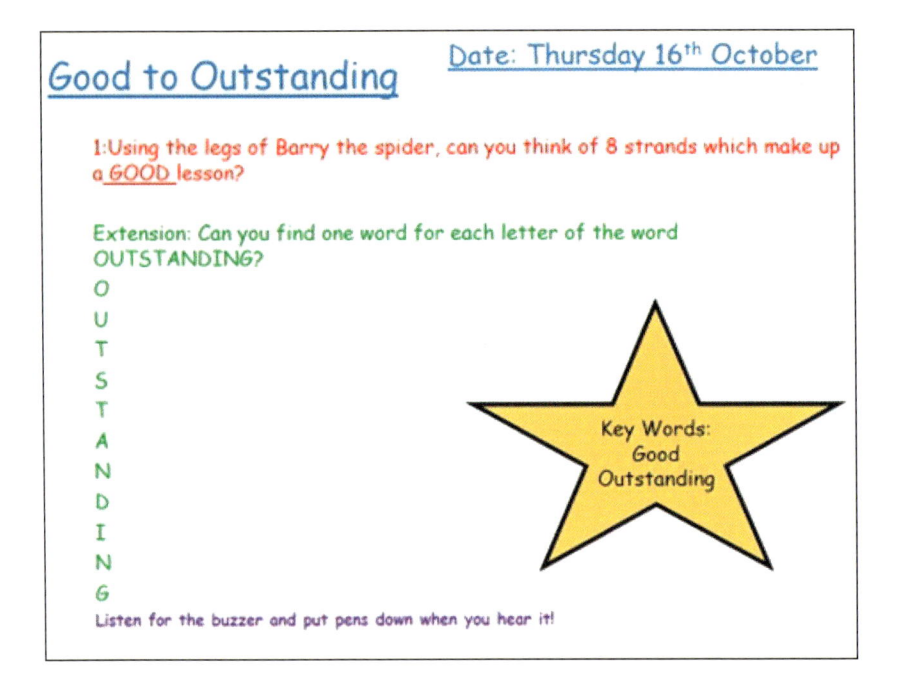

O
U
T
S
T
A
N
D
I
N
G

Listen for the buzzer and put pens down when you hear it!

Key Words:
Good
Outstanding

KQ:
How can I differentiate between a good and an outstanding lesson?
How will I experiment with techniques in my lessons?

# 2. KEY QUESTIONS

**To set the aim for the lesson with skills that are accessible to all.**

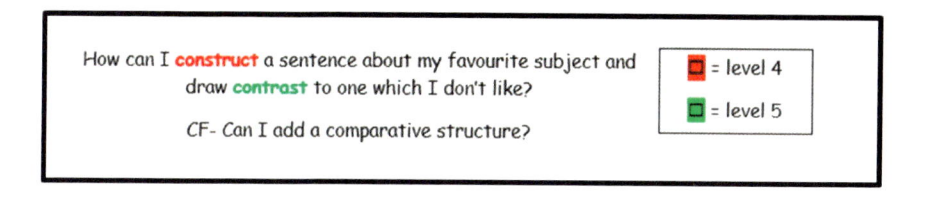

---

How can I **construct** a sentence about my favourite subject and draw **contrast** to one which I don't like?

CF- Can I add a comparative structure?

🟥 = level 4
🟩 = level 5

---

Differentiate key questions to cater for different cohorts. Use differentiated/colour-coded learning objectives/Key Questions using key words from Bloom's Taxonomy in order to develop separate skills.

E.g.    **Define / List / Recall…**
        **Select / Contrast / Explain…**
        **Analyse / Evaluate…**

Have the KQ displayed during the lesson and tell students how they could achieve it: make this measurable!

KQ

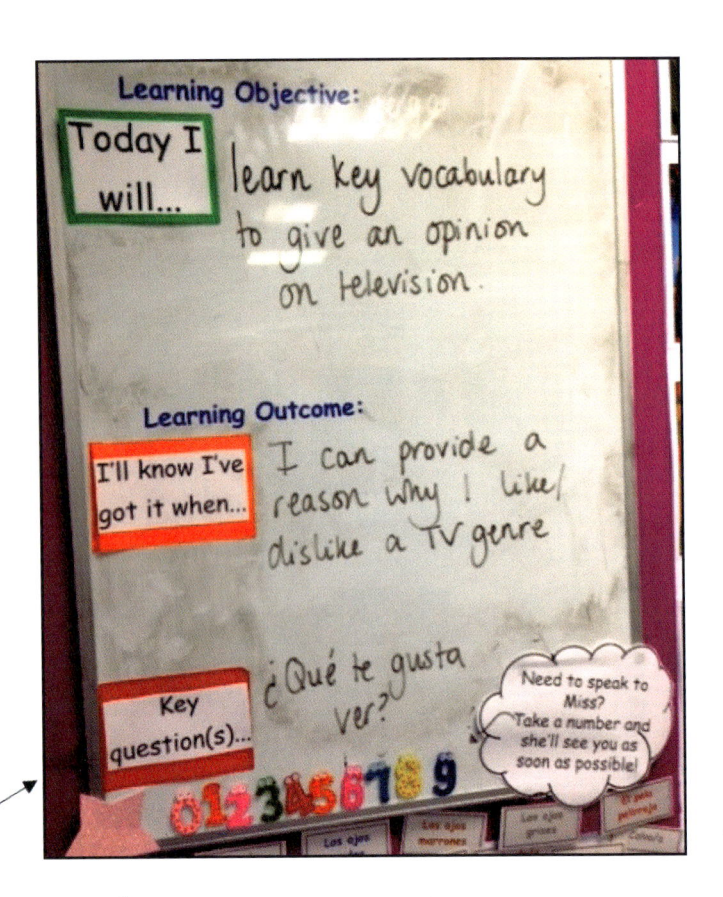

Want students to stop calling out "miiiiisssss" or "siiiiiiir"?!

Have some numbers available that they take and wait their turn to be helped/seen.

# 3. STARTERS

**Something that should engage/settle students. A starter could help introduce a new topic or review prior knowledge.**

If the lesson starts at 09:00, thinking should be taking place the moment they step in your door. Greet them, hook them, make them want to be in your lesson and not want to leave!

Always have something, whether it be a thinking task, written task or reading task ready on the board/desks for students to be getting on with. A quick, positive start sets the scene for the rest of the lesson.

There are of course, hundreds of starters out there in the world of teaching that may be useful to you. Some teachers like random starters that are not linked to the learning of the lesson but personally, I find it more useful to me and the students to set the starter as a recap of the previous lesson or use it as a lead into the new topic.

Have a starter that requires focus and thinking/problem-solving skills to settle pupils down (e.g. odd one out, guess the theme, find the mistake)

- **Register Response.**

Have students answer their names with a word/phrase related to the topic. Make it so that words cannot be repeated or they have to link the previous student's answer to their own or the responses must start with a given letter or perhaps, follow the sequence of the alphabet.

- **Hook students with the starter.**

Whilst it is important to have a KQ/LO, you do not HAVE to start each and every lesson with this. Ask students to stand at the front, by the board, as they enter the room, with a projected picture related to the topic. Ask them to think of a question to ask you about it. They are immediately intrigued because a) they are not having to sit in their chairs and b) they get to ask you a question not just give answers. Make your classroom an environment where it is ok to ask questions. The objective and/or key question will eventually emerge. Just because you are not doing it at the very start of the lesson does not mean students will not see it/"get it"!

- **Text Instructions.**

Anything to do with modern technology engages students. So, set up a fake text and display it on your board with instructions or questions, which they must read and follow.

- **Target Setting.**

After introducing the key question, ask students to set a target for the lesson, written on a post-it note. How will they use certain skills? What level do they hope to achieve? Give each student a number and ask them to stick their post-it note next to their number on a large sheet of paper. At intervals in the lesson, allow them to return to this and add/amend as required. They could do this on the same post-it note or provide them with a different colour to differentiate between ideas.

- **Classifying.**

Ask students to place information related to the lesson into columns, tables or a Venn diagram.

- Mind the Gap.

Provide instructions or topical words in a long sentence with no spaces. Students need to identify where the gaps go and follow the instructions given/note the keywords or find out their meaning.

- Bin it!

Have a grid of words where a certain amount are related to the lesson and others are not. Ask students to find the words that they believe are related to the topic and bin the ones that are not.

- Use pictures to teach the skill of inference.

Get students discussing what the lesson might be about and why? Encourage questioning rather than them worrying about the answers at this stage. If the lesson requires them to write a letter to a tourist office, do not immediately lose their interest by placing huge amounts of text on the board but instead, use an image of a tourist office with clients. Get them thinking: what might the clients be saying? What sort of information are they asking? Are they happy or sad? Make your classroom a make-believe tourist office. Once enough questions have been asked, and ideas have been agreed on, set the main task. Students will be much more willing once they have asked the questions they need and feel confident with what they are doing.

- Predictions.

After introducing the lesson objective or key question, ask students to predict how they will meet this objective/question within the lesson. Review this at key points to add or amend as appropriate, and then a final review could be carried out as a plenary. Did they predict correctly?

- Clues.

Have clues (key words/objects) for the students to try to guess what the lesson will be about and devise their own KQ/learning outcome. Refer back to this at intervals in the lesson, are they happy with their KQ or could they/should they change a key word?

- **Have a dump! / Dump it down! / Empty your head!**

What do you already know about the topic? Dump it down! Ask students to write key words/phrases/ symbols. Tell them that full sentences are not required at this stage and at intervals in the lesson, have them add to their work in a different colour pen or use the word(s) in a sentence to demonstrate progress.

- **Code breaker.**

Devise a code and have students try to crack it to work out the theme of the lesson or the next instruction.

### Code Breaker!

| A | B | C | D | E | F | G | H | I | J | K | L | M | N | O | P | Q | R | S | T | U | V | W | X | Y | Z |
|---|---|---|---|---|---|---|---|---|---|---|---|---|---|---|---|---|---|---|---|---|---|---|---|---|---|
| 18 | 24 | 20 | 4 | 3 | 8 | 7 | 9 | 5 | 25 | 13 | 19 | 14 | 10 | 12 | 21 | 17 | 16 | 0 | 11 | 2 | 15 | 23 | 22 | 1 | 6 |

- 21 / 18 / 16 / 20 / 3    17/ 2 / 3

- 25 / 3    20 / 16 / 12 / 5 / 0    17 / 2 / 3

- 20 / ' / 3 / 0 / 11

- 25 / 3    21 / 3 / 10 / 0 / 3    17 / 2 / 3

- **Family Fortunes.**

Give students categories for which they write five key words. They only get a point if their word matches one you have also thought of. A quick way to get them thinking about key words within specific topics.

> **Write down 5 French words for each of these categories...**
>
> **Colours:** bleu, orange, vert, rose, rouge
>
> **Transports:** train, car, voiture, vélo, bateau
>
> **Countries:** La France, L'Angleterre, L'Espagne, Le Portugal, L'Italie
>
> Try to think of the 5 most popular answers for each in order to win a point! Bonne chance!

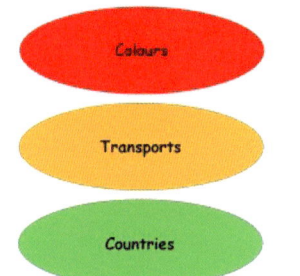

- "Find the Mistake."

Use "Find the Mistake" as a way to address misconceptions from the previous lesson. Teacher to write sentences with mistakes made on purpose. Students must correct them and explain why they have done so. This is not only limited to subject specific information, but literacy could also be incorporated, e.g. the teacher could miss out punctuation for students to correct. This is also an effective technique to use after marking work. If a common misconception is evident, use the mistake as a starter to help re-teach the topic.

- Fake letters/emails/text messages/news reports/props.

Use fake letters/emails/text messages/news reports/props to set the scene for the lesson or a task. Ask for the student's help: "Guys I've just got this email I need to write a letter to the head teacher on what I think of the school uniform, can you help me?" Get them discussing, collating advantages and disadvantages and ultimately, believing that they will help you in your mission.

- Make up key words.

Use random words where students have to take the first letter from each, and then unscramble them to make up a key word from the lesson.

---

### Pour commencer…

- Use the first letter of the English words to discover a scrambled French word. Unscramble the letters to form the correct word (they are all places in a town!)

1) Drum / Elephant / Train / Apple / Snake = s t a d e

2) Sock / Cinema / Igloo / Night / Potato / Indian / Egg =
p i s c i n e

3) Truck / Noodle / Indigo / Orange / Angel / Post / Rabbit / Engine / Insect = p a t i n o i r e

4) Robot / Eagle / Garage / Animal = g a r e

# 4. DIFFERENTIATION

**Provide an opportunity for all learners to learn by setting a variety of tasks at various paces.**

Set up a permanent "Challenge and Help" desk for students to use. If you feel like students may abuse the Help Desk, provide them with a token to trade in order to use the help desk.

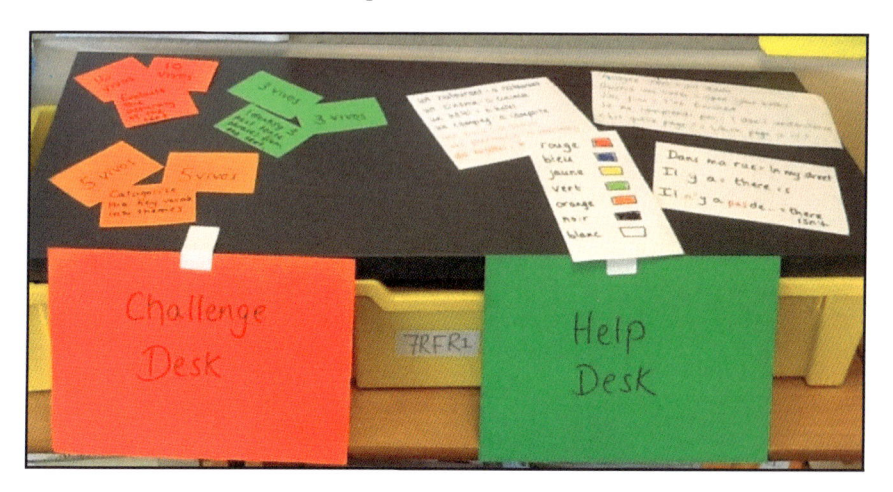

Generic challenges, to suit any topic, could consist of:

- Write a poem/song/rap about your learning today.
- Create a comic strip to depict your learning and understanding.

- Can you summarise your learning in exactly __ words.
- Roll the dice and make the following improvements to your work:

   1 – Check your accents.
   2 – Include two connectives.
   3 – Include a positive and negative opinion.
   4 – Include four adjectives.
   5 – Include a signpost.
   6 – Check your punctuation and spelling.

> The help desk could have specific resources for the lesson such as model answers, criteria grids or a list of key words/sentence starters they could use.
>
> Or, it could be more generic by having dictionaries, textbooks, calculators etc.

Have a **bank of challenge** cards/challenge capsules to stretch the more able as extension work. Challenges could be similar to above or could include tarsias or jigsaws.

I also display challenges on bunting and students can pick which they would like to attempt. Each challenge has a number, and if they attempt one, they must put the number of the challenge in their book with the answer. When marking books, I reward students for their challenge attempt.

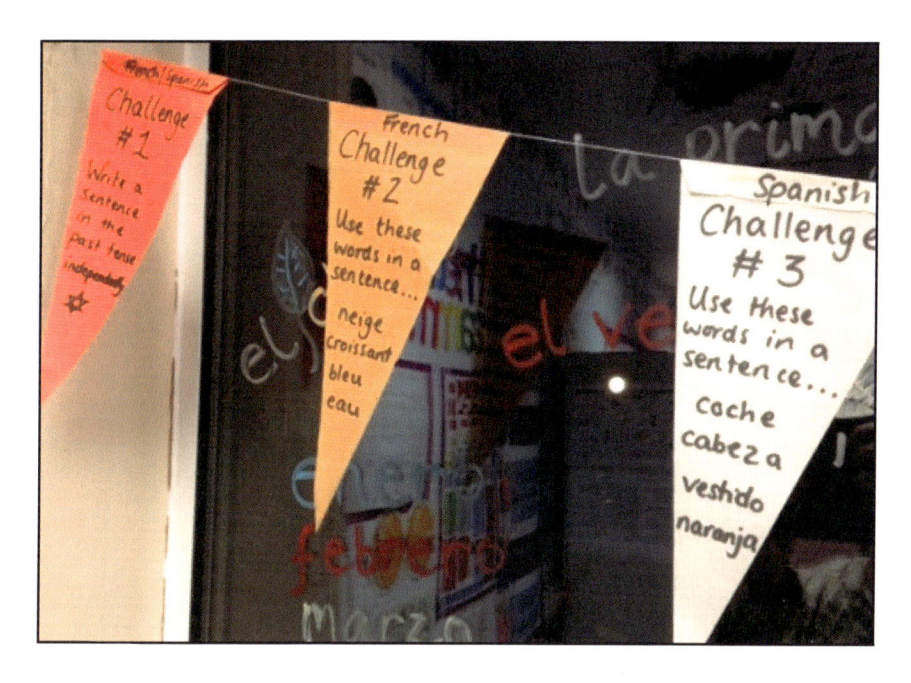

These challenges range from creating sentences, finding new vocabulary or making as many words as they can from a grid of random letters.

| Your challenge, should you choose to accept it…. | Your challenge, should you choose to accept it…. |
|---|---|
| Draw a picture to demonstrate your understanding of the KQ. | Create a starter activity for next lesson. |

> **Your challenge, should you choose to accept it….**
>
> Summarise your learning in 5 key words beginning with "D"

- **Differentiate questioning.**

Differentiate questioning by using a variety of question stems to structure the question or, allow students to self-differentiate by offering red, amber or green questions. Easier questions could result in fewer rewards, encouraging students to stretch their learning

- **Think!**

Have I got all pupils engaged in a challenge factor? This does not have to be the same for all students though, especially when you may be faced with a very mixed ability class. A student with a target of a 4a is likely to have a different challenge to those with a target of a 5a, but all should strive to reach their challenge. Therefore, give differentiated challenges that are tied to levels and provide students with differentiated instructions and roles.

- **Cloze activities.**

Cloze activities can work well for less able students, particularly with writing tasks. Leave gaps for the students to fill in or for even further differentiation, you could provide the missing words at the bottom of the page for students to choose from. Another quick way of differentiating for less able students is to provide multiple-choice options.

With listening and/or reading activities, provide students with a grid to complete, e.g.

| A (must) | B (should) | C (could) | D (Challenge Factor) |
|---|---|---|---|
| TV programme | Opinion | Reason | Additional information |

- Clue cards.

Point students in the right direction with this support device. Provide selected students with a bank of vocabulary or statements related to the topic or clues on how to answer the questions set.

This immediately provides them with a gist, and they become more confident with what is expected of them in the task.

Differentiate by assigning different tasks to students based on ability. Therefore, the tasks should be varied in complexity or the skills required to complete it.

---

### Romeo and Juliet

• After I've given you a letter, think about the task...

**All the As:**
What do you think is the purpose of the character Paris?

**All the Bs**
If you were to redirect the film. Who would you cast as Romeo and Juliet? Explain why.

**All the Cs**
How would you update the play to make it more current? Where would you set it? Why?

---

Give small groups a list of activities/tasks they should complete. Each member of the group MUST complete one and while the teacher could distribute tasks based on ability, students could also naturally self-differentiate based on their individual skills. One task may involve using single vocabulary whilst another may be forming short paragraphs.

### 5 points

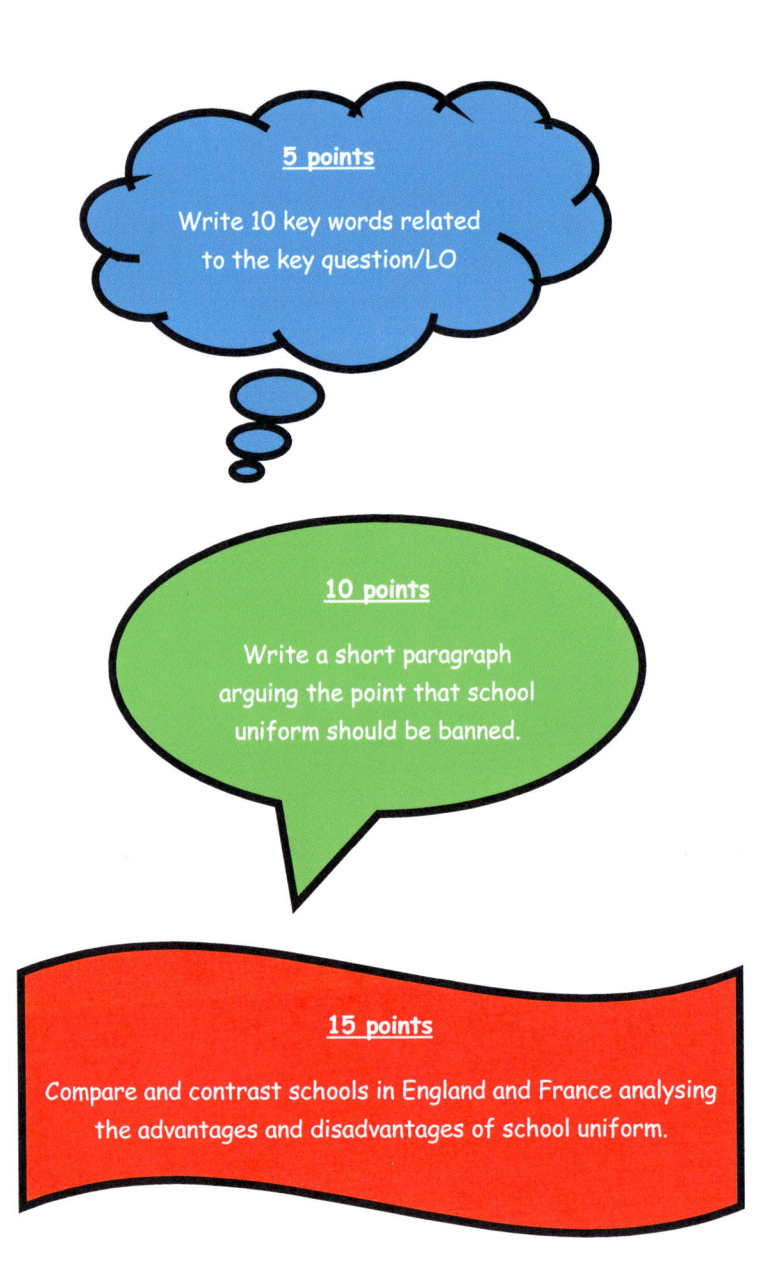

Write 10 key words related to the key question/LO

### 10 points

Write a short paragraph arguing the point that school uniform should be banned.

### 15 points

Compare and contrast schools in England and France analysing the advantages and disadvantages of school uniform.

# 5. AFL TECHNIQUES

**A means of deciding where students are at in their learning and where to go next as well as how to get there.**

- Using Success Criteria.

How do you expect students to meet criteria if they are not told what it is in the first place?! Imagine… I have asked you to draw a dog, but I have given no more information than that. Would you ask questions of what I expect? Most probably. You might ask what breed of dog? What colour? And, if you need to draw a collar or lead. Had I of said to you that you can only get full marks if you were to draw a dog bowl next to the dog, you would probably be upset because you did not know that. Not giving students criteria is the same thing, and they are less likely to achieve high grades/levels if they do not know what is expected of them.

- **Formative Feedback**. (Marks and grades alone do not tell students what they need to do to get better)

Marking or verbal feedback needs to be evaluative but descriptive at the same time. Do not just say "Well Done" to a student, say "Well Done; that answer was great because you managed to include a variety of connectives."

- Effective questioning.

Use a bell/whistle/signal to indicate question time. This could be teacher questioning or send a message to students that it is time for them to devise a question based on the lesson.

- **Swag Bag.**

At the start of the lesson, ask students to draw a bank (the kind where you save your hard earned cash!) in their book and "deposit" any words that they already know related to the objective/key question. At intervals in the lesson, ask students to add to the bank as more content is taught. I ask students to use a different colour pen when doing this to clearly differentiate between what they knew and what they know now. In addition to this, allow a form of peer assessment/teaching to take place and ask students to swap books and discuss the key words in their different banks. When books are passed back, ask students to draw a robber with a swag bag. In the bag, they must place any "stolen" words from a partner and as the lesson progresses or as a plenary, they should try and link bank words and swag words together to avoid jail.

Alternatively, if you do not want them to peer assess, just have them place new words in the swag bag after you teach them more lesson content. If they think a word is important, they can choose to "bank" it in their bank but must use all words in their bank by the end of the lesson.

- **Peer, self-assessment and evaluation.**

This has a great impact but in order for it to be successful, it must be standard classroom practice not something that is done once in a blue moon. For more strategies on this, please see the section on marking/responding to marking.

- Pupils setting their own targets. They will need to know criteria for this but ask them to set a target and at intervals in the lesson, get them to comment on their learning journey towards this target.

- Ask students to highlight how they have met the KQ/LO for the lesson.

- **Pit stops.**

To be used on a regular basis so that students get into the habit of summarising/feeding back on their learning. Have a logo/sound or gesture that signifies that it is time for a pit stop/mini-plenary. I have used a pit stop in almost every lesson from the first day I stepped into a classroom and now, as soon as my classes hear the word pit stop, it is a moment of pride for me because quite simply, they look forward to it. In fact, I could never forget to do one because half way through the lesson books are automatically closed, pens are down and they are ready for question time, ready to summarise their learning, ready to let me know of any misconceptions out there. I have always and will always use pit stops as an opportunity for students to earn rewards based on their understanding/participation and in my classroom, students get to "up" their points.

Three years ago, I put up a basketball net in my class and during question time, if students got an answer right, they had the chance to "up" their reward by having a shot in the hoop but only if they answered a more difficult question to the previous one or, added to their previous answer. If they scored a basket, points were doubled, if they missed, a point was lost. Some teachers have argued that this is not learning, and points should not be taken away. You might agree. However, it is teaching the students to take risks, and it is encouraging them to be effective participators and since then, other methods of "upping" points have been introduced.

I now also have a dartboard where they aim for bull's eye, I have cards where they have to guess if the higher card is on the left or right hand and I have a die that is rolled to try and obtain the highest number. Students roll it once and can stick with what they get or roll it a second time, and if they achieve higher, they get that amount, but lower means they lose everything.

The students **LOVE** these and they are an excellent way to consolidate learning and get them considering how much they know/can share. Learning does not have to stop whilst "upping" takes place as the teacher can be directing other questions to the class, or they can be devising their own questions for each other.

---

### Pit stop moment!
- Add one key word to your margin to summarise what you've learnt up to this point!

### Question time!!

What's the French for "I went"?

Why is there sometimes an extra "e" on "allée"?

How do you say "it was great"?

Translate on whiteboards- I went to Germany, it was boring.

Add a signpost to the sentence above to improve your level.

---

Use pit stops as an opportunity to question students, bouncing answers where possible.

Also, allow this time to address misconceptions and re-teach strands of the lesson if necessary.

If a TA is present, ask them to direct a question to the class or comment on their understanding.

- General questioning.

Do not let students be put off by giving a wrong answer. Use this as a means of addressing common misconceptions by taking the time to re-teach a part of a topic. Additionally, allow students to bounce answers, phone a friend or offer them a 50/50. Furthermore, rather than ask a very direct question that makes students feel like there could only be one answer, e.g. "What does profit mean?" Use the word "might" to put them more at ease, e.g. "What might profit mean?" This allows for a wider scope of answers and students to help one another build on responses.

- **The good, old, mini-whiteboard.**

    A quick way to see the whole class feedback at a glance.

- Get them to draw their thinking/answers or ask them to translate your words into pictures.

- Get them to answer in silly ways, e.g. "write with your eyes closed" or "write with your left hand if you're right-handed" and vice versa.

- When asking them to share answers, ask them to all hold their boards up on a number or with their eyes closed. This minimises the amount of copying from partners or changing of answers if they feel they are in the minority.

- **Pass the whiteboard.** A variation on pass the parcel that extends thinking/answers by asking students to assess each other by correcting mistakes or adding to answers.

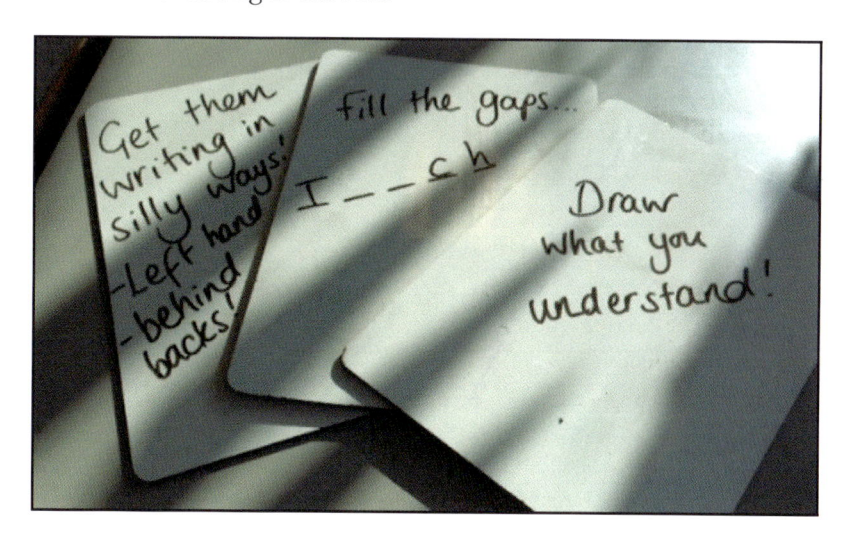

- **Ask the audience.** Pose a question and have students vote on whiteboards. One side of the whiteboard could show answer and the other side could explain their reason for choosing this answer.

- **Key words and definitions.** Ask the class to summarise a stage of the lesson/part of the topic in a keyword or create a definition for the lesson.

- **Fill in the blank.** Teacher calls out a sentence/sum and students must display the missing word/number on their whiteboard.

- Different colour pens.

At intervals in the lesson, get students to swap to a different colour pen and add to their work after having taught different elements of the topic.

Get students to RAG key words from the lesson. This could also be taken further by getting them to use words in a sentence, e.g. "Rate the following words from 1 -3":

1 = I remember seeing this word!

2 = I could tell you what this word means!

3 = I could tell you what this word means and use it correctly in a sentence!

You would then check this through questioning.

Different colour pens also work well as **Peer Assessment**. Each member of the class has a different colour. After setting the task and students working on it individually, have students peer assessing work based on criteria given. Students then give the work back to the original student who must work on their feedback. Another way of doing this is with highlighters. Set a key for the class, e.g. yellow = connectives, orange = time expressions, blue = negatives, and so on… Ask students to peer/self-assess using this key. At a glance, they can then see what their strengths are and/or what they are missing!

- **Student becomes the teacher.**

As a plenary/mini-plenary, ask a student to come and teach what they have learned/understood from the topic. I used just to listen to them but now, I actually take the place of that student and raise my hand to ask questions to extend their explanation. I love this activity because not only do they show you what they have understood but it is also great fun watching them mimic your teaching (from this, I realise that I say "okay" a lot!) and you get to be the student for a short period of time. My favourite thing to do, during this exercise, is give them a taste of their own medicine and often just state "I don't get it". Their frustration at trying to explain it in a different way, whilst annoying for them, is a great teaching method because it is challenging and stretching their thinking and communication skills.

- **Pass the parcel, with directed questions or exam questions.**

Wrap questions between layers of newspaper or, for a quick fix, place them in a box/bag, not as fun for the students, but it means less preparation. Students pass the parcel to music. Once the music stops, a question is pulled from the box or unwrapped, and the student answers the questions. Reward answers or if not quite correct, or more could be added, pass to the next student/volunteer. Using this method, students will eventually piece together a whole answer.

- **First attempt.**

Before teaching any content of the lesson, display key words on the board that will come up during class and ask students to draw a table in their books with two columns. One column is to be labelled first attempt and the other, actual answer. Ask the students to write what they think the word means in column one or how they think it will be used today. As the lesson progresses, ask them to refer back to this table. Were they right with any? What could they add in now that more content has been taught? An alternative to this, particularly if studying a text is to ask students to label the columns with "From My Brain" and "From the Text". Get them to fill in the brain side first and see if anything matches after they have studied the text. Were their assumptions right? This gets the students predicting and ultimately thinking deeply about what they are studying rather than just being spoon-fed.

- **Post-it notes.**

A must-have in any teacher toolkit as they can be used in so many ways. They can quite simply be used as a means to answer the KQ by sticking them on the board at the end of a lesson and used as an exit pass/ticket or as a way to make amendments to work on a second draft.

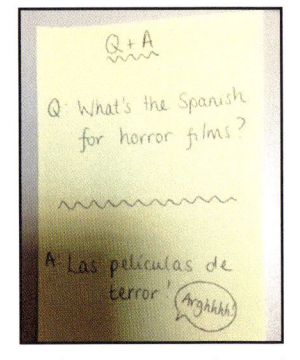

However, they can also be used by dividing the post-it in two. The top half should indicate how they could answer/meet the KQ/LO before the lesson is taught and then the bottom half to be used as a plenary: what can they add/amend/redraft after the lesson has been taught? You might also like to try having two different colours of post-it notes whereby one colour is what they hand in when they answer the KQ/LO and the second colour is used for either any questions they might have (have a dedicated space in the classroom where they can place these during the lesson and give students a chance to respond to these. This could be as a pit stop or calling on an "expert") or anything they could add to someone else's answer. Finally, post it notes can be used as a means of Q&A. Students could create a question at the end of the lesson and as a starter in the follow-up lesson, they circulate the room or sit in lines, facing a partner, asking their question and listening to answers. They have the opportunity to correct or improve their partner, and then they switch. After both have conducted a Q&A session, they swap cards and go to a new partner. This strategy allows students to peer teach and build up a bank of knowledge.

If teaching different elements within one main topic, e.g. the main topic is food but within that, you would like students to learn different vegetables, fruits, snacks and drinks. Place the main headings on paper or the board, leaving enough space underneath for students to place post-it notes, stating something they have learned within this sub-topic.

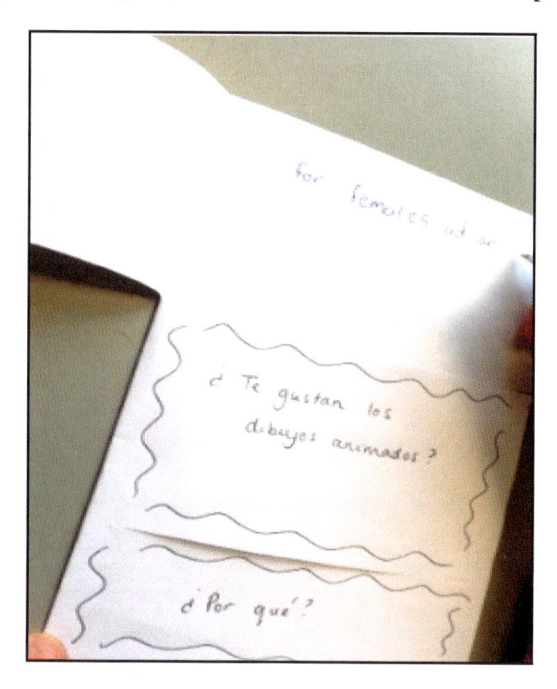

Put a key question/some key questions on a sheet that has been cut to allow students to write the answer underneath. Teach your lesson as normal, giving information/key ideas/words on how to answer each section.

As a mini-plenary, have students creating answers to these set questions. Through this pit stop, as students share ideas, they can add to their answers.

This is an ideal way to check learning as well as show progress at stages in the lesson.

Use the starter as an opportunity for students to place previous knowledge/what they already know against the key question and learning objective.
As the lesson progresses, ask students to add new knowledge to the board in order to demonstrate what they have been learning.
As a plenary add a post-it to the section-what do I need to find out/need to know next?

Start with a basic mind-map with students noting key words based on the KQ/LO or inferring from a photo.

As the lesson progresses, using a different colour pen get students to add ideas to their mind-map, which develops their learning and skills.

As the lesson progresses more and more ideas should be added.

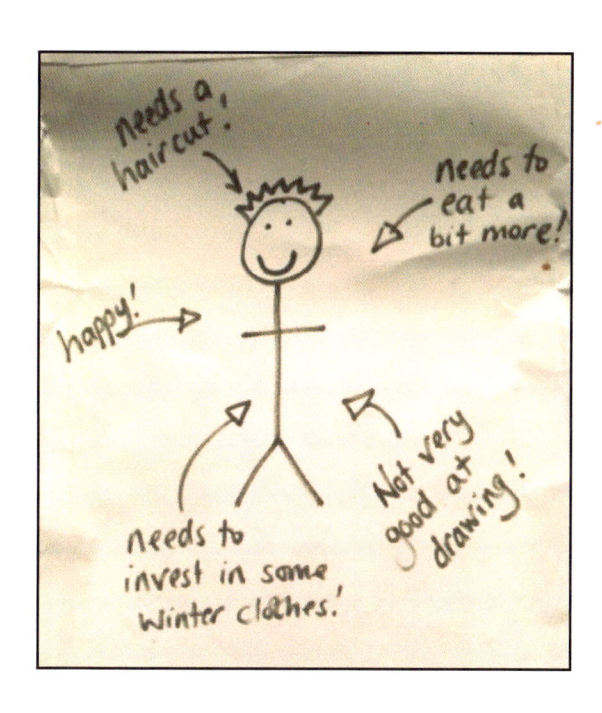

- **If this is the answer, what is the question?**

Write a model answer to an exam question or the key question and ask students to decipher what the question might have been. As an extension, if using an exam answer, ask them to decide how many marks they think the exam question was worth. This can also work with placing a picture/key words on the board and asking them to make connections to what the objective might be for the lesson or designing the key question.

- **Exact Words.**

Giving students a mini whiteboard or a space in their books works well for this. Ask them to summarise their learning in an exact amount of words. They cannot go above or below the number given. The amount of words could vary each lesson, and students should aim to summarise their strengths, weaknesses or what they believe to be the most important part of the lesson.

- **Abstract thinking skills.**

Encourage students to really think about their learning by placing a "thunk" or a shock question on the board. For example, a lesson on equal opportunities could start with the statement "All the boys in this class have homework this week. The girls have none." Students should automatically start to discuss (boys will kick off!) the statement, leading into discovering what the lesson content is about.

- **Model My Learning.**

Using modelling clay, have students demonstrate their understanding of key words by creating a model/sculpture to show the meaning. A twist on this is to take a small piece of clay away from any group/individual who sculpts a wrong answer, cannot explain their modelling (especially if it is not easily identifiable). In addition, you could ask students to model their feelings towards the learning.

- Tell Me, Show Me, Draw Me...

Rather than have students simply write what they have been learning, ask them to show you through different mediums. This could be through drawing, miming, signing, freeze frames, maps or sculptures. The different methods allow you to see how they have interpreted their learning and encourage different forms of communication.

- Life Cycle-Learning Cycle.

Have students imagine that their learning is like a life cycle. Ask them to show you/explain to you which stage they are at, e.g. frogspawn to frog or seed to flower. They should identify the stages in between and link them to their learning. Students should be able to explain why and how they are that particular stage of learning. Additionally, as the lesson progresses, and students become more confident, frogs could go and help tadpoles, and tadpoles could help frog spawn!

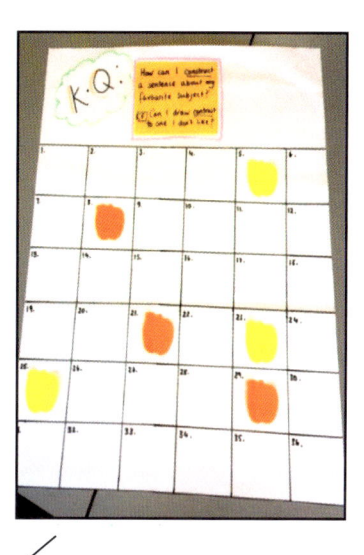

> Number each student in the class. After the KQ/LO is introduced, explain to students that throughout the lesson, they may come and stick a post-it next to their number with answer to the KQ as long as they feel confident to do so.
>
> Teacher could then plan in a mini-plenary and address some of the answers given. This could allow for progression in the lesson in terms of stretching or addressing any misconceptions/common errors in relation to the KQ.

- Musical Marking.

Ask students to write a list of information based on a topic or question (I get mine to write on tables with washable markers for ease of correction). Once completed, tell the students that they will now circulate the room whilst some music is playing. As soon as the music stops, they need to find a new table and circle any mistakes in the original list, placing their name or initials next to it. However, they are NOT to correct them at this stage. Repeat this a few times with students visiting different desks. Ask students to then return to their original desks and review the mistakes circled. Can they identify and correct where they went wrong? If not, give them the opportunity to go and speak to the person who flagged up the mistake and engage in peer teaching.

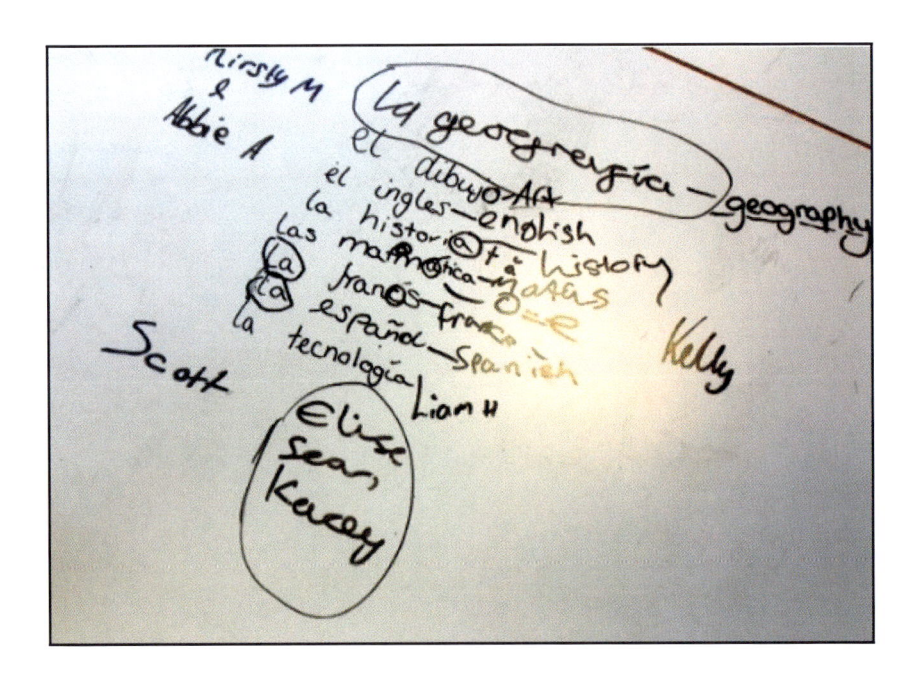

# 6. QUESTIONNING

Use this as a means to test the effectiveness of your teaching as well as assess the student's understanding. Your classroom should be a place where it is ok to ask questions.

1. Which is better?
   A - "Ethan, what is the meaning of divertido?", or,
   B - "Ok class, what is the meaning of divertido?"

- Answer = B. By doing option B, all of the class are more likely to listen because it could be they who have to answer the next question. Picking only one student before the question is asked is a way of making sure that everyone else in the class is relaxed… and that is not what you want!

- Asking the question before choosing someone to answer also ensures that students are engaged throughout the lesson, as they are wary of having to answer questions. Also, avoid giving the reward before the question is asked. By stating that the next question is worth 5 points, automatically puts some students off of answering because the points are not enough for them to get involved.

- Vary the way in which students answer questions, e.g. fastest hand first, hand up only when they hear a multiple of a number/connective and at times, have a "no-hands up" policy. Random name generators/lolly sticks work well for this or simply ask a student for a number and count the names down the register. I often ensure that they are all listening by stating that they can only raise hands once they hear me say the word "go". I then call out words such as "going", "gone" and "gorilla" before actually saying, "go" to keep them all engaged. You can see the intensity at which they are listening for the key word in their faces, and how they are poised and ready to pounce!

- Vary the way in which YOU ask questions and allow the students to pose questions to you about the task. Do not just ask the basic "What should we do/can we do?" Challenge students by asking, "What shouldn't we do?" Your questioning should cover all strands of Bloom's Taxonomy ranging from recall to understanding, applying to analysing and evaluating to creating.

## 2. Build in wait/pause time before allowing students to answer. (This should be at least 3 seconds.)

- Encourage students to wait by a) not allowing shouting out, and b) after the question has been asked, count the hands going up in the air. You will be surprised how many more hands go up if you say "Oh, only three hands so far!"

- Do not feel uncomfortable about waiting for responses. If you feel more should participate, use the wait time to rephrase the question/give hints on how to answer or allow students think time before responding by jotting down key words or taking the time to share an idea with a partner.

## 3. Call on all students in the lesson at some point. (This could be to answer a question in front of the whole class or a directed question during a task.)

- Ensure that all students have equal opportunities to participate in the lesson and try to get one response from each student per lesson. I often have a whole section of the lesson where students are not allowed to raise their hands and must be ready to provide some form of answer if targeted. I also use the phrase "Who haven't I heard from today?", and I target the students who have not yet participated. Create a class competition whereby every time a student answers a question they put a tally mark in the front of their books. At the end of each lesson/week/half term, award the best participator with a reward or title of "Perfect Participator".

- If a student is not quite sure of the answer to a question posed, allow them to phone a friend, think, pair, share or have some extra individual thinking time. Make sure you tell them that you will call on them again later to find out the answer but do not forget to do so! Place a post-it note on their desk so they can formulate an answer and hand it in to you once they feel confident.

## 4. Encourage some form of response by providing hints/tips and having a backup.

- If they are taking a while to respond, never be tempted to answer the question for them. Tell the student that you will give them a bit longer and come back to them or try re-phrasing the question/have another student word it in a different way.

- Direct students to wall displays/sections of textbooks or their own notes to help formulate an answer. Additionally, I often give the role of a "spy" in a lesson and allow students to spy on other groups/pairs/students to help them give an answer or complete their work. Furthermore, if you see a student is struggling to provide an answer, give them a set amount of time to use resources to help them. I often say, "OK, 30 seconds to look back at your notes" or "one minute to search in a dictionary". This helps them feel more confident and takes away the pressure of answering on the spot.

- Do not allow the students to just pass on a question with a simple "I dunno!" Use this as an opportunity for students to phone a friend, have a 50/50, use a clue or alternatively, let them ask if the question could be re-phrased or if they could have time to think about the question or have a different one.

- Assess confidence and understanding levels by setting targets when posing questions. If asking a sequence of questions state how many students out of the class you would like to get each one right (obviously you would always like all of them, but it is rare that this happens) and place the target on the board. Ask students to note responses and then peer assess. The results could lead to including numeracy in your lesson by working out percentages or creating a graph. To boost student's confidence, why not try betting with them? (Not that I condone gambling, of course!) e.g. "I bet less than half the class will get this one right." Of course, they will do anything to prove you wrong so will try their hardest to succeed.

## 5. Allow them to learn from their mistakes and feel good about it!

- Never publically embarrass a student and although sometimes their answers are completely wrong, try to find some good in it and praise that part, e.g. "Not quite the right answer but you were on the right lines with the word xxx."

- If mistakes are made, do not let the student give up. Ask further, leading questions to set them back on the right track.

- If they make a mistake but a peer helps them out or they find the correct answer from hints/sources etc. ask them the same question again nearer to the end of the lesson so that they do not have the lasting memory of getting it wrong. As they say, we learn from our mistakes!

- Have differentiated questioning using strands from Blooms. Where possible, have pre-prepared differentiated questions in a red, amber and green box. Allow the student to pick which box they would like their question from, e.g. green box questions might start with "recall a key word/fact from the lesson", amber box "explain the meaning of xxx" and red "justify your opinion".

- Get students practising their poker face by posing a question to the class. Anyone can raise their hand, regardless of if they are confident of the answer or, even know the answer. Pick a student to answer; if they know it, everyone else who raised their hand, including them gets a point. If they do not know the answer, no points are given, or a point is deducted from all who raised their hands. Follow this up with further questioning to try to elicit a correct answer.

Have a variety of question types in the lesson:

Specific (closed) - To be used when a student needs to give a factual/specific piece of information. "What is the capital city of Brazil?"

Thinkers (open) - This encourages higher level thinking skills and an expansion on specific information. The question may include the basics of what has been covered in the lesson, but gets students explaining their thought process. "If the world spoke only one language, what language would you choose and why?"

Discussion makers - Start by posing the question to the whole class as a form of voting, e.g. yes/no, true/false, this/that then select individual students to go into more depth, provoking discussion/debate. "How many of you think learning a language is important?" John: "Can you explain why you think this?" Sasha: "As you haven't raised your hand, can you explain why you disagree with John?"

**Guiding** - To be used when the teacher wants to guide the students to an answer. "If all regular past participles of –ir verbs end in "i" then "fini" is regular, isn't it?" This could then be followed up with extra questioning to extend independent thinking.

**Interest makers** - To be used to engage students in the topic or get them back on track. "If an earthquake were to occur in Clacton and you were at home but had to evacuate, what would be the first thing you'd save and why?" Challenge students by asking, "What wouldn't you save?" "Why?"

**Eliciting Answers** - Pose a question to students and have multiple-choice answers on the board to which they hold up mini whiteboards to show answers or have answers placed around the room and they have to go to the one they think is right. Use further questioning to encourage students to justify their answers. The justification could be carried out by one member of the group standing at each station or, give the group time to formulate a justification together. This could then be used as a method to try to persuade other groups that their answer is correct and rewards could be given to the most convincing group.

**Think Before You Speak!**

Allow thinking time before answering questions by using a variety of methods:

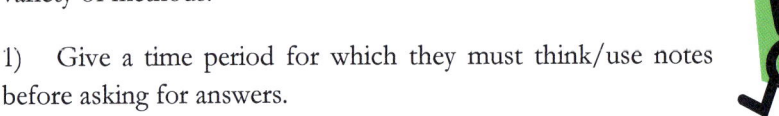

1) Give a time period for which they must think/use notes before asking for answers.

2) Ask students to mind-map ideas in pairs before turning to another pair to share ideas and then feedback to the whole class.

3) Ask students to write down at least three key words/phrases before answering and reward extra points for "working out" as well as their answer.

4) Allow students time to "spy". This could be through reviewing notes in their books, using textbooks/dictionaries or spying on a partner's work.

**Encouraging Reasoning.**

- Try wording questions in different ways to challenge learners and get them stretching their thinking.

- Instead of asking a question that requires a simple yes or no or a specific answer, e.g. "Is 'vendu' a regular or irregular past participle?" Ask them to explain the meaning, e.g. "What does it mean for a past participle to be regular or irregular? Can you give an example?"

- Avoid factual recall by asking questions like "Why is Oxygen a gas?" "Why is 'jouer' a verb?" or "Why is A an example of B?"

**Find the Answer.**

- To consolidate understanding on a topic or, to introduce a new topic, provide half the class with questions and the other half with answers. Have students walking round the room, discussing matches and finding their partner.

- This could be followed up with extension questions, asking students to explain the reason for their match.

- A variation on this is to have only a third of the class with questions and two-thirds with answers, some of which should be incorrect, encouraging students to discuss the correct option. The group of incorrect answers could then create a question to match their answers. Alternatively, have two correct answers for one question or two questions for one correct answer. All of these techniques promote discussion and thinking skills amongst students.

- Use post-it notes for this exercise or mini whiteboards. Post-it notes could simply be held by students or placed on their foreheads or backs to make the exercise more interesting! With mini whiteboards, again, students could walk round with them, or the answers could be hidden under tables/chairs, etc.

# 7. MARKING/RESPONDING TO MARKING

**Effective feedback should be useful, specific and timely, and students should be given enough lesson time to act upon it.**

Giving students a "Well Done" is great for their self-esteem, but do they know what has been done well? Therefore, this kind of feedback should always be accompanied by more descriptive marking, e.g. "Well Done, your use of the connective 'and' to link the two ideas together is great. Next step, use a higher level connective in your next piece of work such as 'however'". This type of marking informs the students of what they have done well whilst implying how they can reach the next level by adding improvements (AfL).

Remember, you do not have to mark everything! Keep WWW/EBIs related to the KQ/LO. Also, if the marking is not going to be effective for the student, why do it? Consider marking as a means of intervention, differentiation and a means to inform your planning. If common misconceptions are occurring, it might be time to re-teach a particular element of the lesson.

- **Ideas to help students engage with marking:**

- Highlighting in red, amber and green. Anything that stands out as good = green, improvements = amber, items needing a full correction = red.

Ask students to respond to these in the lesson or as a starter/plenary.

- "Check your dot" - ● A quick fix to marking in lesson is to highlight errors whilst circulating the classroom and remaining silent. This could be done with a simple highlighting pen or by placing a mark (dot/star) next to their work. They must then respond to this in the lesson without your input. Therefore, you are highlighting the error but, by remaining silent, you are not giving them the reason why it is wrong, and they are using problem-solving skills independently.

- Have students self/peer assess against clear, concise criteria. Students could create this criterion themselves, or it could be teacher/exam board generated. They could tick off/highlight what they find in their partner's work, therefore, making anything un-ticked an area for improvement.

- If you have similar sets/abilities, swap books with each class or another teacher and gets students to peer assess the books based on set criteria. This cross-class marking also encourages healthy competition among the groups as they can see the strengths/weaknesses of a similar ability set.

- Mark half the class and use those as models for the class to mark the other half through peer assessment or, if you have access to a visualizer, project a piece of marked work on the board for students to use as a guide.

- Use a piece of work as a model and have students gather round for critical analysis. They can discuss WWW and EBI (with you guiding them), which can then be written down as verbal feedback. Then, have students go off in small groups/pairs to do the same.

- If marking a writing task, split the class into three. One set is to be marked by you, with some of the more able students watching how you mark and giving suggestions, another group to be self-assessed and finally peer assessment to take place in the last group. This could then be extended through a carousel activity of adding feedback to the marked work if possible.

- If the same task has been set to the whole class, flick through all books and see if there is a common mistake among them. If so, use this as an opportunity for students to re-draft their work after you have taught them how to improve. They could put in their books that it is a re-draft based on VFG (verbal feedback given). Students should follow this up by explaining what feedback was received and how this improved their work.

- Try to mark in the lesson. If you are setting a written task, try to go round with a green/red pen in the lesson, highlighting any key errors/WWW. Once you have marked, students can immediately start working on their EBI.

- Ask the children to review and mark their own work before it is handed in. This is a very effective way of encouraging your students to reflect on what they have done. Ask them to identify where they would particularly like some feedback.

- Give students a different colour pen to your marking colour and set a routine for this. Set a routine whereby different colour pens mean different types of marking, e.g. green = teacher/TA, red = pupil response to teacher marking, purple = peer or self-assessment. This can take a while to set up but is invaluable once it is.

- Ask students to tick your comments in their colour once they have read them to show acknowledgement. This also encourages them to respond to anything that requires a response. Have symbols to represent improvements needed, e.g. circle any spelling errors, underline any grammatical errors, highlight any targets met, etc. Give the criteria colour codes where possible and get students to highlight where they have met it.

- Use two different colour highlighters as teacher marking or self/peer marking. Anything green (or another colour of your choice) is what has been identified as a strength. Students should then follow this up as why it is a strength/what they have understood well. The other colour should highlight any areas for improvements and the next step should be a re-draft so that they demonstrate recognition and understanding of feedback but have also responded to it.

- Provide students with a gap fill exercise to consolidate the understanding of key words or lead on to the next topic. You could give a clue to help, e.g. "What is the word for a financial gain, especially the difference between the amount earned and the amount spent in buying, operating or producing something?" Students would fill the gaps to find the word: _ _ _ _ _ _. This could be differentiated by completing some of the gap fill with letters or providing different clues based on ability. To encourage students to engage in **literacy** through marking, try a similar technique to the above whereby students fill the gaps to practise their incorrect spellings. The hangman style activity helps them to keep the correct spelling in their long-term memories, and an extension could be given to finding the meaning of the key word.

- Rather than correct spelling, punctuation or grammar yourself, simply highlight errors in the work and ask students to work on these as a starter/plenary.

- Give students a list of key words on a post-it note that have been identified as incorrect and ask them to re-write them correctly.

- Ask the students a question and make it explicit. Do not give students an excuse for ignoring it, so, draw them a box in which they should write their answer.

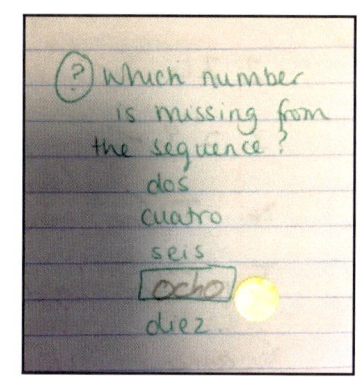

- Encourage students to demonstrate their independent learning by giving a CF (challenge factor) that extend the lesson and their understanding. Again, provide a box in which they should respond to this. I have found that having a visual box for students to place their answer encourages them to respond. This can be varied by different sized boxes: use a small box and get students to write in their smallest writing or a certain number of boxes should indicate that a certain number of words should be used.

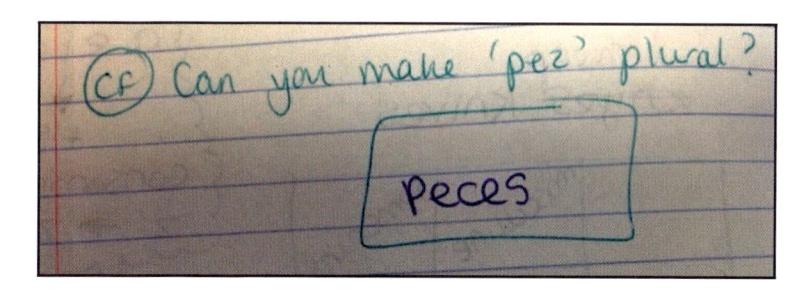

- Encourage pupils to 'talk' to you via their books. Instead of making comments, ask questions: "Why did you choose this word…", "How could you improve…?" or "Is ___ correct?" And in return, they can ask their own questions, make points of information or clarify misunderstandings and assumptions.

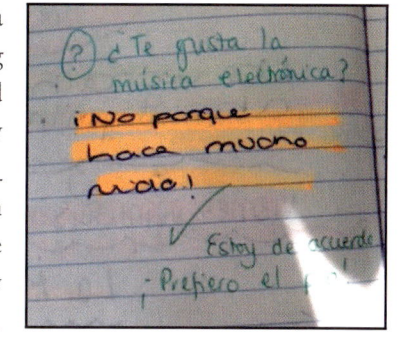

- A technique I often use in marking and as a starter activity is asking students to find mistakes in my marking to demonstrate their understanding of the topic. Making these purposeful errors stretches their thinking, and you could extend this further by asking them to explain why it is incorrect, consolidating their learning.

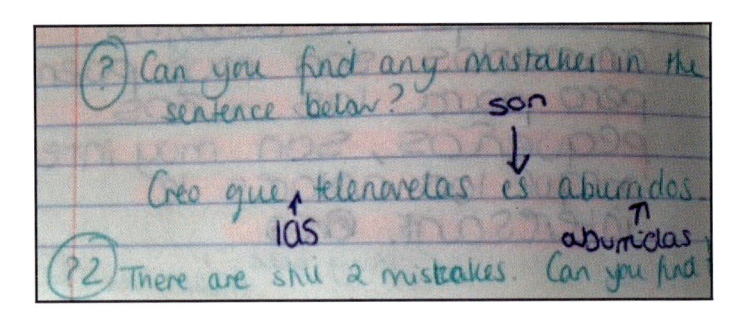

- **Peer/Self-Assessment**

    Although this is often completed in lessons, it is not always explicit to an observer who flicks through books for a couple of minutes! I once was marked down in an observation because although I had SA and PA in the books, the small code for this, on the side of the margin, was not clear enough! Therefore, I would suggest you make sure that you regularly use this technique and evidence it in student's books so that it is easy to see, at a glance!

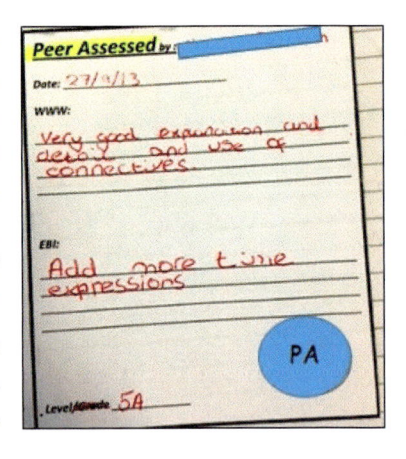

- Have generic peer assessment sheets to hand that could be printed on a different colour paper or have a symbol or logo.

```
┌─────────────────────────────────────────────┐
│  Peer/Self Assessed by:_____       │
│                                             │
│  Date: _____              │
│                                             │
│  WWW:                                       │
│  _____        │
│  _____        │
│  _____        │
│  _____        │
│                                             │
│                                             │
│  EBI:                                       │
│  _____        │
│  _____        │
│  _____        │
│  _____        │
│                                             │
│  Level/Grade _____                  │
└─────────────────────────────────────────────┘
```

- Have a bank of possible WWW/EBI statements for the students to get used to and eventually they will start writing like you! It just takes time. I used to hate self and peer assessment because I would end up with statements like "WWW = you have neat handwriting", "EBI = you finish all the work". Students were not actually commenting on the task in hand but after persevering with it and using examples to start, students can now write mature and useful feedback. Carry out peer and self-assessment at least once a week and make it part of your standard classroom routine.

> Use stickers where possible to reward good work or highlight mistakes.

**WWW=**
- Excellent presentation of work ☐
- Fantastic understanding of the key concept/words ☐
- Your determination is outstanding! You have addressed mistakes and learned from them ☐
- Your hard work means you have beaten your target level/grade ☐

**EBI=**
- Please improve presentation of work by keeping handwriting neat ☐ underlining dates/titles ☐ using all space/pages ☐
- Please use textbooks/dictionaries to deepen your understanding ☐
- You need to put in some extra effort and determination in order to reach your target ☐

| Spelling | Punctuation | Grammar |
|---|---|---|
| **Consistent** spelling of **key words**, e.g. place names/famous people's names ☐ | **Correct** and **consistent** use of **full stops** at the end of each sentence ☐ | **Clear** and **structured** paragraphs ☐ |
| **Correct** use of **homophones**, e.g. there/their/they're ☐ | **Correct** use of **speech marks** ☐ **apostrophes** ☐ **commas** ☐ **question marks** ☐ **speech marks** ☐ and/or **exclamation marks** ☐ | Use of **complex sentences** through a **variety** of **connectives** e.g. because/consequently /moreover, which join together words, phrases and clauses ☐ |
| Use of **Standard English**. No text speak, e.g. u/lol/ur! ☐ | There are **capital letters** at the start of each sentence and for all proper nouns ☐ | **Variety** of **synonyms**. These are words that have a similar meaning to another word. We use synonyms to make our writing more interesting ☐ |

- Creating generic tick lists of criteria is a quick way for all types of marking. To extend this further, mount students work on A3 paper and have them draw arrows to where they have met each strand.

Data is also useful in marking but I was always trained not to give students simply a mark out of ... or a grade. The reason being is that it is not useful to them in terms of progression. Therefore, if you are going to give a mark, make sure it is backed up with descriptive marking about how they achieved that and where to go next. Or, to make this type of marking more effective, mark work with a grade and description but keep the grade in your mark book.

Provide students with descriptive feedback only and then display levels and grades on the board with a brief description of how they could achieve each one. Have students assess which level/grade you would have given them and why and see if they match up to your marking. This has far more impact than simply giving them the mark outright because it gets them thinking about HOW they have achieved.

Just as a teacher should have their data to hand, students should also know what level they are working at and where they can go next.

| Last assessment_____ | Last assessment_____ |
|---|---|
| This assessment_____ | This assessment_____ |
| I feel_____ | I feel_____ |
| because_____ | because_____ |
| I am happiest with | I am happiest with |

Last assessment_____

This assessment_____

I feel_____

because_____

I am happiest with

- I display my student's target levels or grades on the inside of their books, and they refer back to these before and after an assessment piece or any other levelled piece of work. Different coloured target cards indicate how the student is doing, and I provide them with a space to record their progress and comment on it. Have these sticking out the top or sides of books so that it is evident to an observer.

- Furthermore, it is important to remember that all feedback should be **positive**, **specific** and **useful** and it may be worth having sheets made up or a wall display to model this, which provide the students with sentence starters.

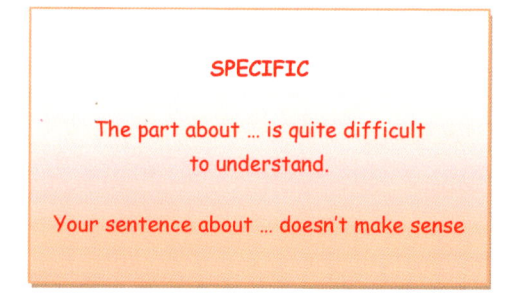

> **POSITIVE**
>
> Excellent ..............
>
> My favourite part was ...
>
> I enjoyed the part ...

> **SPECIFIC**
>
> The part about ... is quite difficult to understand.
>
> Your sentence about ... doesn't make sense

> **USEFUL**
>
> Try adding ...
>
> To improve, remove the ...

- The wheel method promotes self and peer assessment and ensures that students are assessing based on specific targets. Around the outside of the wheel, place criteria related to the task. After a task has been completed, ask students to judge how effectively they have achieved each strand within their work, rating them from one (I have done well and have a variety of examples to prove it) to five (not present within my work). Students should use a different colour for each strand and then use this colour to highlight the examples in their work. Ultimately, this allows them to see, at a glance, their strengths and weaknesses and provides an opportunity to respond to marking.

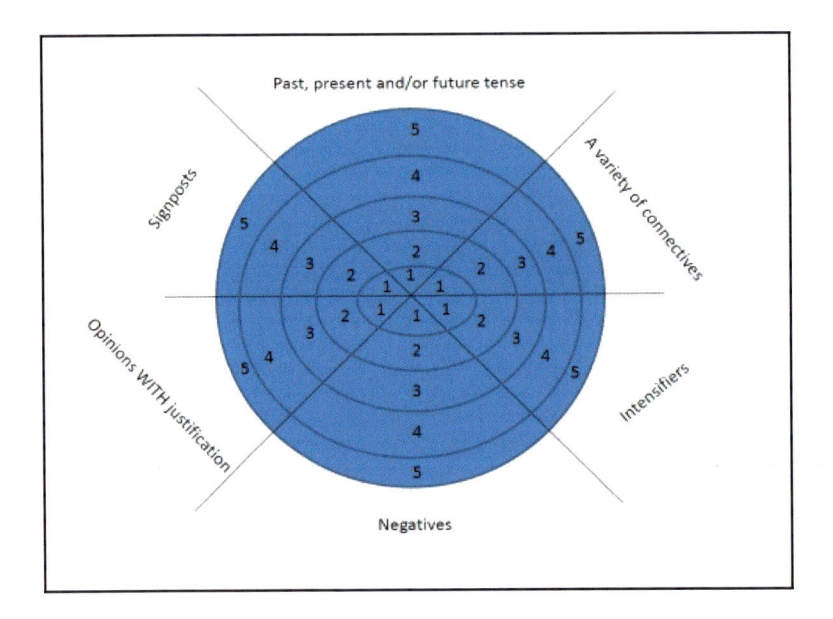

If I am completely honest, I dislike marking. I am convinced that books multiply whilst they are sitting, waiting to be marked, and it is the one part of teaching that I would get rid of if I could. For me, it is a bit like going to the gym, the build up to it and getting there is a chore but once you are there and finished, you do feel much better for doing so. Marking is, undoubtedly the best form of differentiation, intervention and planning. However, for all of the above methods to have any impact at all, getting students to respond to marking **must** be as soon as possible. Students should not be expected to remember feedback for a week the same way that if you mark books, they should respond to your marking the very next lesson to get the best responses from them.

Effective written dialogue between teacher and student is an example of outstanding practice, but routines and expectations must be made clear, and asking students to respond to marking must be a regular activity. Additionally, as you are asking them to take the time to respond to your marking, you should also go back and acknowledge their response and ensure that understanding is correct. If it is not, ask further questions or set further tasks. Marking should be used to **support** students, **challenge** them as well as **consolidate** learning.

- **Support** - This is aided by having wall displays/help sheets that are given to the student to help them in making improvements. "Good try; now use the grammar wall to help you with your present tense verb endings."

- **Challenge** - This encourages the students to put their learning into practise independently and whilst the question should still be based on the main topic of the lesson, it should stretch their thinking skills: "Great! So now, think about how much material you'd need to make twice as many samples."

- **Consolidate** - This marking encourages students to try a few more examples or explain their learning before moving on. The questions posed or EBIs given should draw upon errors previously made by students or where you write an incorrect sentence and ask them to identify the errors or improvements, e.g. where a student has failed to link sentences with a connective, you give the feedback of "Well Done, you've justified your opinion well now, what could you use to connect the two sentences together?" Or, here is my sentence (written by the teacher) "I like peas and carrots. I don't like ice cream. Whilst I've given an opinion, how could I make this sentence better?"

This photo shows a plenary activity whereby students had to work in teams to create a sentence by passing the pen to one another, continuing the phrase. I could see that mistakes were being made and therefore took this photo and projected it on the board during the next lesson. As the starter activity I split the class in half again and told them how many mistakes there were and asked them to identify them. Although this was not marking in books, it did generate a great learning conversation amongst the students.

# 8. INCORPORATING LITERACY AND NUMERACY

| LITERACY | NUMERACY |
|---|---|
| Only raise your hand to answer the question when you hear a connective/verb/adjective etc. | Only raise your hand to answer the question when you hear a multiple of 7/prime number/ odd number, etc. |
| VCOP displays/literacy mats, which are referred to in the lesson | If you got 7/10 spellings correct, what is that in a %? |
| Have students read silently for a period in the lesson or read aloud whilst other make key notes. | Present your findings from a survey in a graph/chart. Differentiate the graph type based on ability. |
| Ask students to write out figures in words. |

- Place a range of numbers on the board with certain numbers missing. Students need to sequence the numbers and work out where and what the missing number(s) is/are. Get them to write their explanation in their books using connectives to sequence what they did and when.

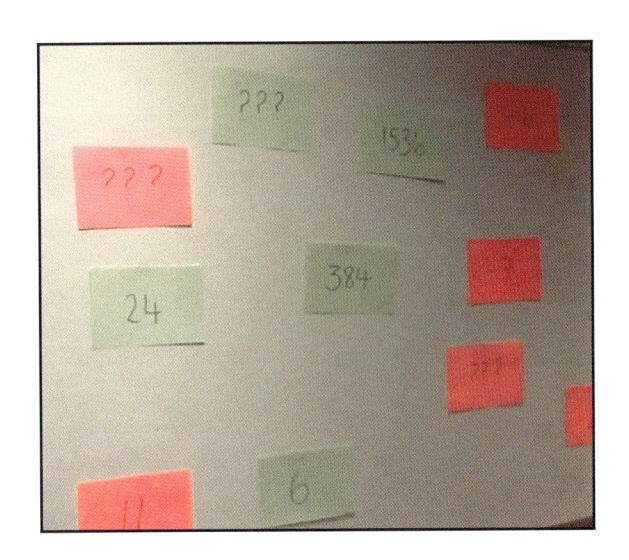

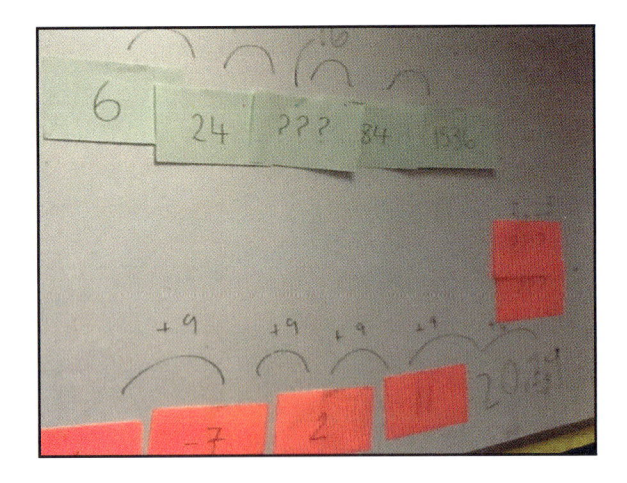

- **Spend the Words.**

    Connectives/verbs/adverbs/nouns, etc. all to be given a monetary value. The more complex the word, the higher the value. Students aim to spend as much as they can, keeping a running total of their spending in their book. Biggest spender to be rewarded.

### Spend the words!

se trouve (£1.00)
dans l'est (50p)
de l'Angleterre (£1.00)
c'est (75p)
historique (25p)
située (£1.50)
dans l'est (50p)
touristique (25p)
environ (£2.00)
très (£1.50)
À ___ kilomètres de Londrés (£2.50)
habitants (£1.00)
si vous aimez (3.00)
il existe (£1.50)
nous avons (£2.50)
vraiment (£2.00)

---

If each letter is worth 2p, can you devise a word to state a skill you've used today with a word value of above 15p?

(Remember: you can use a letter more than once)

**CF** - Can you find a key word from the lesson that costs EXACTLY 32p?

**A B C D E F G H**

---

- Tension graphs in novels based on emotions/feelings of characters or where tension is at its height throughout the book.

- Confidence graphs/tables. Students to plot a graph or complete a table during specified intervals in the lesson.

| Aim | Beginning | End |
|---|---|---|
| I know the difference between un and una. | ☺ 😐 ☹ | ☺ 😐 ☹ |
| I can name at least 5 different items of school equipment in Spanish, from memory. | ☺ 😐 ☹ | ☺ 😐 ☹ |
| I can apply a connective to my work to make the sentences flow. | ☺ 😐 ☹ | ☺ 😐 ☹ |
| I can use "tengo" and "no tengo" to describe what I have in my schoolbag. | ☺ 😐 ☹ | ☺ 😐 ☹ |
| I can recall the Spanish alphabet from memory with approximate pronunciation. | ☺ 😐 ☹ | ☺ 😐 ☹ |

- Have an extract from a novel/textbook/source displayed on the board with a variety of numbers at the bottom of the board: one of which should be the answer to the clues you will give. Within the text they should count and find the total number of verbs (or other category of your choice), they could then divide this by the amount of full stops then add the amount of metaphors to that answer. Other equations could be given but by the end of it, their workings out should lead them to a final answer that matches to one of your given numbers. This takes a bit of preparation, but it is an effective and challenging way to get students engaging with a text and using their numeracy skills.

| A | B | C | D | E | F | G | H | I | J |
|---|---|---|---|---|---|---|---|---|---|
| 17 | 10 | 0 | 8 | 48 | 34 | 27 | 100 | 4 | 79 |
| K | L | M | N | O | P | Q | R | S | T |
| 23 | 84 | 2 | 18 | 29 | 21 | 7 | 76 | 97 | 19 |
| U | V | W | X | Y | Z | Space | | | |
| 45 | 6 | 14 | 31 | 68 | 101 | 74 | | | |

2014 - 1985 =

7 x 3 =

88 - 12 =

8 x 6 =

> Work out the sums to find the corresponding letter. You'll then need to rearrange the letters to find the connective we're looking at today.

- Use literacy and numeracy boards to present a focus and dedicate a space in your classroom for these skills and other resources to challenge students. Example: Use lolly sticks with key vocabulary and challenge students to make a sentence. Have a word of the week displayed in the class and reward students if they use this in their work. Alternatively or in addition, have a random number displayed in your room/on the board and challenge students to write something in the lesson, which is that exact amount of words.

# 9. SHOWING PROGRESS / PROGRESS OVER TIME

**Keeping a record of progress will evidence it!**

Assessment tracking sheets are a way for the students and the teacher to see progress-over-time at a glance. You could develop sheets for individual assessments and colour code them with highlighters or post it notes or you could create a sheet, which allows students to record all of their assessment results on one sheet with dates, name of task, target and level achieved. To extend their assessing skills further, you could include a space where students also record a statement about what they have done well and how they aim to improve next time. Get this signed by the student and yourself and place it in their books for reference.

If a task does not link to the learning, and allow students to make progress against the LO / KQ, do not do it! Make everything that you do a step to success, which can be demonstrated at intervals and the end of the lesson. Try to chunk lessons into 10-minute blocks, reviewing the learning at the end of each stage.

Assessment Title: _____

My Target Level is:

| Level | Assessment Criteria | Example |
|---|---|---|
| 3 | I can state what *I like and dislike*, linking my sentences using connectives and talk about more than one thing. | |
| 4 | I can incorporate a *signpost*, talk about somebody other than myself and I can give a reason for my opinion. | |
| 5 | I can incorporate an *intensifier* and a negative. I can also use another tense besides from the present tense. | |
| 6 | I can write in *longer, more complex sentences* with a wider range of vocabulary, incorporating present, past and future tenses. | |
| 7 | I can incorporate *complex language and structures*. I can also write and speak spontaneously and accurately. | |

WWW -|

EBI -

Level achieved: _____

 

I started teaching by simply thinking that showing progress was placing a chart/graph on the board and asking students to put a post-it note with their name against the level they were at, at the start and end of the lesson. However, I soon came to learn that progress checking in this format is not accurate. The reason for this is that most students are likely to copy a friend or put their level higher than the start because they do not want to seem like the one in the class who has not learned anything! Therefore, I now use some of the following techniques to monitor and assess progress within the lesson:

- Mind Map.

After setting the KQ/LO: ask students to mind map generic features related to the KQ/LO: what do they already know? As the lesson progresses, ask students to add to this mind-map, in another colour to demonstrate what they can now add to their initial thoughts. Ask them to use a different colour to identify anything they would like more information on and use this as a form of planning.

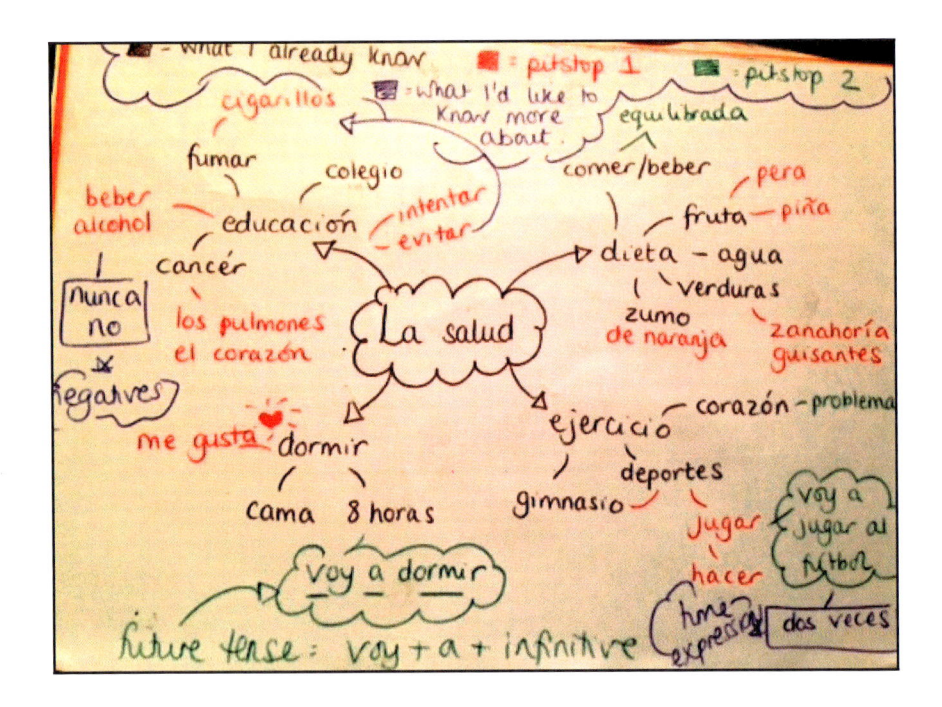

- Pie Chart.

Track progress through the lesson using a pie chart. At the start of the lesson, ask students to note anything they already know/can link to the title/KQ/LO. At intervals in the lesson, ask students to add to their chart with new knowledge and use the plenary to get them to note any questions they might have. You could then use these as a starter next lesson or have students circulating the room during the plenary, adding answers to questions asked. I often do this by allowing the students to use a washable marker on the tables so that a larger amount of information can be added and any misconceptions can be rectified without having to cross out work in books. We then take photos of these and print them out to stick in workbooks or use as a display.

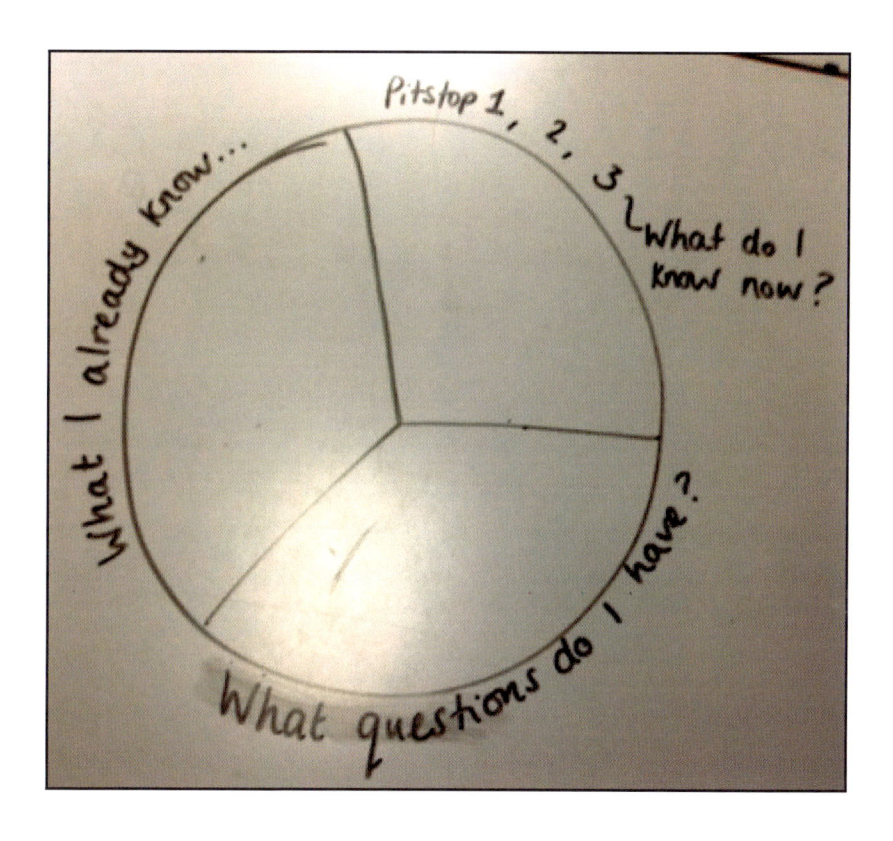

# What do I already know?

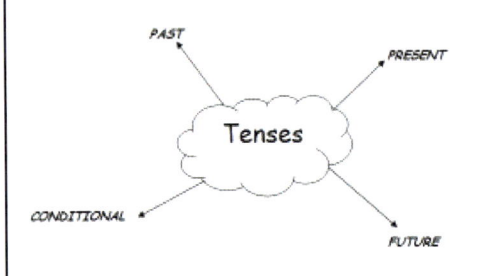

PAST
PRESENT
Tenses
CONDITIONAL
FUTURE

1) What does the tense signify?

2) Do I have an example in English?

3) Where do I put these words?- Infinitive and past participle.

---

# What can I add?

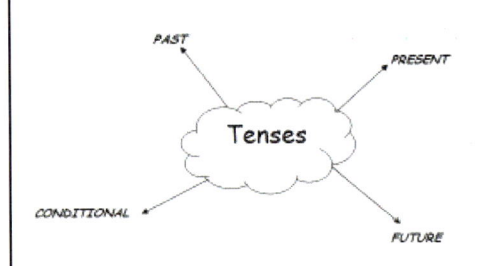

PAST
PRESENT
Tenses
CONDITIONAL
FUTURE

Add me a sentence, in French to your answer sheet, in box 1. You must use one of the tenses we are looking at today!

1) What does the tense signify?

2) Do I have an example in English?

3) Where do I put these words?- Infinitive and past participle.

4) What's the difference between avoir and être?

5) There's only one type of future tense in French. Right?

- Txt A Question.

The "txt a question" method can be used in a variety of ways. Personally, my favourite is to provide students with a post-it note and tell them that at some point in the lesson, they must "txt" a question about the topic, which will be used to question peers. The question can be about something that they are confident about and wish to test others or something with which they need further clarification. As the post-it notes build up, you could stop the class for questioning and as they are answered, move them to the side of the phone. If they remain unanswered, they stay as "un-read" messages and you may need to re-teach an element or address misconceptions until they can be successfully answered. During pit stop, I also like to give students the option to answer a question from their peers or from me, and more often than not, I get a good mixture of the two.

Alternatively, the phone method can be used for students to ask questions to you as the teacher at points in the lesson or as a plenary. Do they have any misconceptions? Could they note what they would like to find out next lesson? These could be addressed as a whole class, or if they put their names on the post-it, you could go and speak to them individually in the lesson or use them as a starter. Picture messages could also be sent by asking students to summarise their learning through a picture/diagram and sending it at the end of the lesson. Finally, the phone could be used as an "ask the expert" technique. Tell your more-able students that they are operating the call centre today and should try to answer any questions asked during the lesson. This could be done by having them write on the back of the post it, or having two different coloured post-its one for questions and the other for answers.

- Progress Line.

Place criteria on the board in sequence of when it should be done. For example, I have completed my mind-map, I have planned the structure of my essay, I have written my opener, I have included at least two connectives, etc. As students complete each of these, they could move a post-it note along the line. Of course, you would need to follow this up with questioning or mini-whiteboard activities but it gives students responsibility for their own learning.

- Sequence of Drawings.

Ask students to demonstrate progress by a series of drawings in the lesson. Pose a question at the start, e.g. what was school uniform like in 1935? Start teaching key elements of the topic and at stages within the lesson, ask students to review their initial drawing, modifying where necessary. Compare the results as a plenary, asking students to self-assess. What did they do well?

- The Journey.

Use their lesson as a journey and get them to map this out, adding key information to "bus/tube/train" stops as various elements are taught.

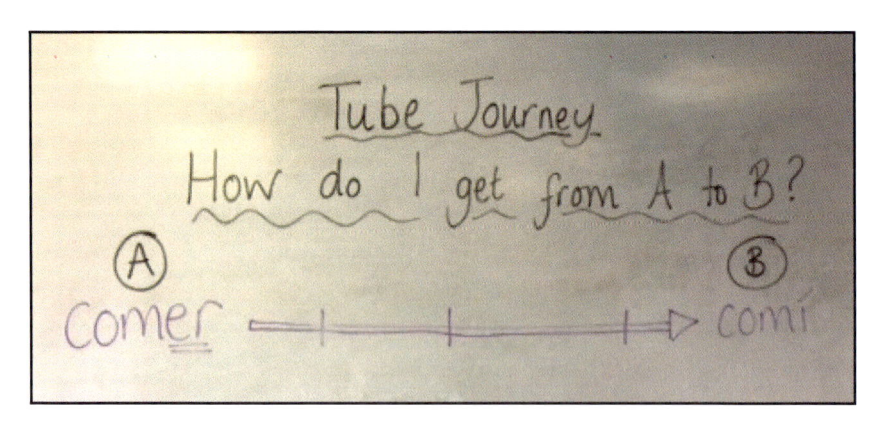

- Progress pages.

When teaching a topic, have students add new words to the middle pages of their book and as they use them throughout the lesson or follow up lessons, allow them to circle them, noting where they have used them, e.g. see essay on xxx for evidence.

- **Bingo.**

Use a 3 x 2 grid, either pre-prepared by you or created by the students. As the lesson starts, ask them to place what they think is the most important word from the KQ/LO in box one. As the lesson progresses, during pit stop one, ask students to place what they think has been a key word within the lesson up to this point, which word stands out for them? Have them write this in box two. Continue with this at three other intervals in the lesson so that they have a total of six words in their boxes. As a plenary, call out the words that you have considered the most important and students cross them off if they also have them. The first to get all six words should be rewarded.

| Construct | Opinion, e.g. me gusta |
|---|---|
| Connective, e.g. pero | Justification, e.g. porque ... |
| Contrast ... odio | Adjective ... aburrido |

- **Kinaesthetic progress**

At the start of the lesson, before teaching a topic, have statements based around the room. Ask students where they stand on the issue, and they move to the corresponding statement. As the lesson progresses and you have taught more on the topic, ask students to change bases if they feel they need to/can and use questioning to elicit reasons as to why they have moved/not moved.

> I have no opinion because I know nothing about the topic.

> I disagree with the idea/concept because...

> I agree with the idea/concept because...

> I am both for and against because...

- **Key Words/Symbols/Equations on the Board.**

Place key words/symbols/equations on the board as a starter and get students to rate how well they know the item, e.g. 1 = "I have no idea what this means.", 2 = "I've seen this in previous lessons but couldn't use/explain it on my own.", 3 = "I know what this means and can successfully explain how to use it with an example."

As the lesson progresses and you teach these structures, have students review their work and re-rate if necessary. Evidence should be given with examples to demonstrate clear progress.

- **Progress Stop.**

Display an image of a racetrack on the board and ask students to use this as a guide to reflect on/comment on their progress at various intervals in the lesson.

**Stage 1** - The start line: what do they know already?

**Stage 2** - First bend (pit stop 1): what can they add?

**Stage 3** - Half way round the track (pit stop 2): what else can be added?

Do they have any questions?

**Stage 4** - Final bend (pit stop 3): How can they start to piece the information together?

**Stage 5** - Finish line (plenary): How can they answer the KQ or address the LO?

Students should record this in their books as a means of AfL and, of course, identification of progress in the lesson.

- **Progress Boxes.**

Always use pit stops as a chance to demonstrate progress but vary the way in which you do this with students. Students can of course demonstrate understanding to you through questioning and mini-whiteboard responses but, if you are being observed, an observer misses this if they come in after you've done it and the lesson shows no real evidence of it having happened. Therefore, having something tangible for the students to fill in after the teaching of each stage provides a resource for them and something for the observer to see, regardless of which stage of the lesson they come in to. Progress boxes could also be differentiated by either having a title for each box, giving students a clue about what should go here or leaving out the clues to encourage students to think about sequence and word order.

(subject)

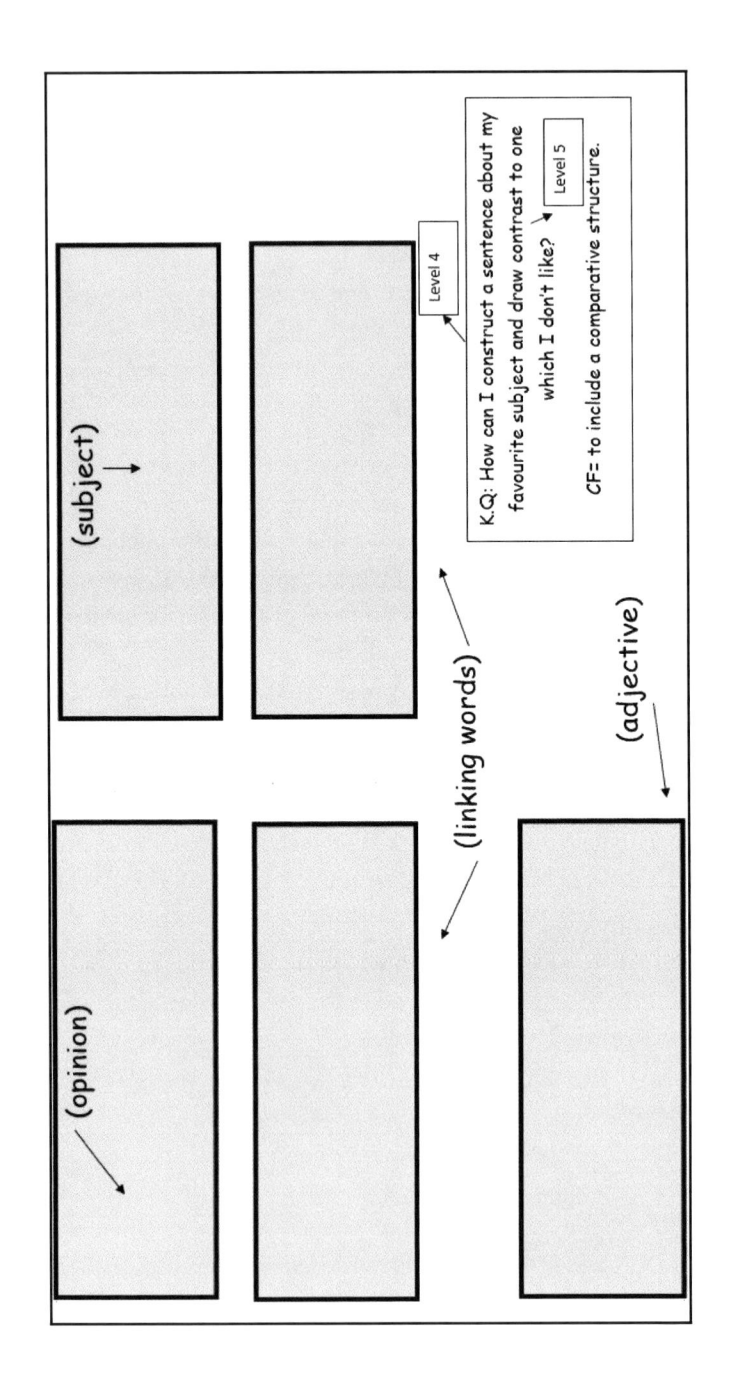

(opinion)

(linking words)

(adjective)

Level 4

Level 5

K.Q: How can I construct a sentence about my favourite subject and draw contrast to one which I don't like?

CF= to include a comparative structure.

**What do I think the aim of today is?**

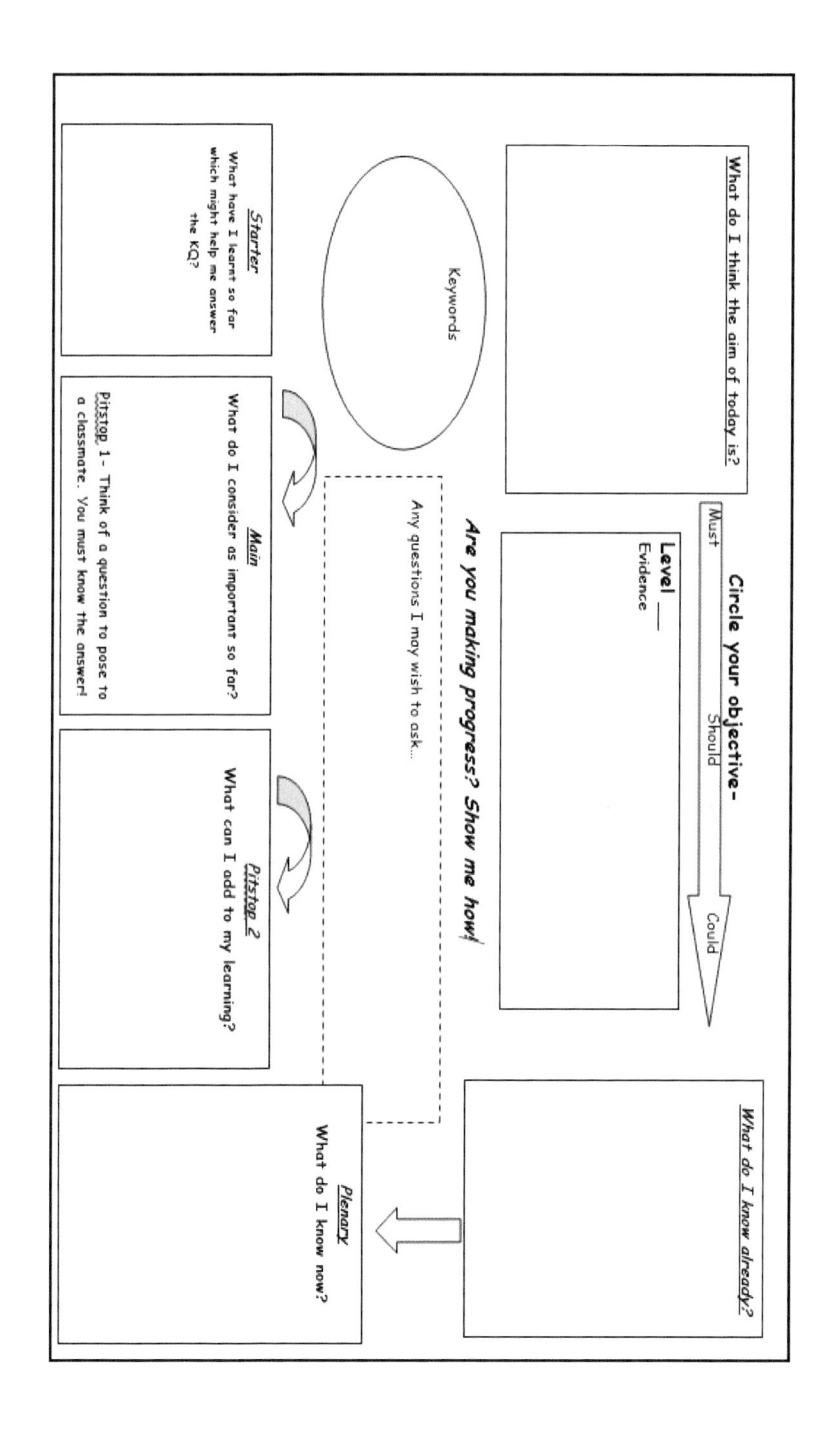

**Circle your objective** -
Must — Should — Could

**Level** ___
Evidence

*Are you making progress? Show me how!*

Any questions I may wish to ask...

Keywords

**What do I know already?**

*Starter*
What have I learnt so far which might help me answer the KQ?

*Main*
What do I consider as important so far?

*Pitstop 1* - Think of a question to pose to a classmate. You must know the answer!

*Pitstop 2*
What can I add to my learning?

*Plenary*
What do I know now?

71

# 10. CO-OPERATIVE LEARNING/ ACTIVE LEARNING

Students are always responsible for their own learning, but we should also promote group work and encourage them to work collaboratively in order to reach a common goal. Students should interact with each other and learn to work in a variety of groups.

- Getting into groups.

In order to group students, you could give some students questions and the rest of the group, numerous possible answers to a given question, e.g. "What would you put in a fruit salad?" One student could have apple, whilst another has orange and so on. Students should discuss the answers and form a group based on their theory. Alternatively, you could have a few photos, which are cut into pieces. Students should circulate the class, seeing if their pieces match up, ultimately forming a group once all pieces have been put together.

- Getting into groups #2.

Give students stickers (white label stickers) in a variety of ways. Cut the label in half and have half the word on one part and the rest on the other. Students then need to find their partner. Vary this by breaking words into syllables for more able groups. Alternatively, give some students key words and others the definition, or give numbers on one sticker and the full written version of the number on another. For History, split the stickers in half with dates on some and events on another. Get students into learning partners/groups by finding matches.

- Verbal tennis.

In pairs, students say a key word related to the topic or string a sentence together. Student "A" starts and then student "B" needs to respond with a new word/next part of the sentence. Students who hesitate could lose a point to try to encourage forward thinking.

- Trading questions.

Ask students to formulate a question based on the topic and write it on a post-it note with the answer underneath. Students then need to circulate the room, asking their question to peers and teaching them should they not know the answer. They then are asked a question back and students trade cards and repeat the process. This method not only gets them speaking and teaching but also acquiring a bank of knowledge.

My question:

Answer:

- Throw your answer!

At an interval in the lesson, have students formulate a question for peers on a piece of paper. Have them screw this piece of paper up or make it into a paper aeroplane and ask each side of the room to throw their questions to the other side. If they can answer the question, they should now answer it on the sheet and throw it back for marking. If not, they will need to go and discuss with the other side of the room to try to find who wrote the question and therefore who can help them with the answer. Another variation of this is to have one side of the room formulate questions and write them down but the other side of the room **THINKS** of a question but only writes the answer to the question. Have students trade paper and either answer the set question or create a question based on the answer given. With this task, I also like to set a challenge for the class where they have to try to beat my target and reward them if they do. For example, when summarising a new topic, I ask students to write as many key words as they can remember. I tell the class that I think they will achieve 10 key words in total but I will only accept them if they are spelt correctly (literacy link!) and I will not accept any repeats of words. They then have to screw their paper up, and I give them a box to try to get them in. I only accept the paper balls that are successfully thrown in the box.

- Musical mind-maps.

The students write their name on a sheet of paper and the topic word in the centre. Students then create a mind-map round the word thinking of all the points they can which relate to this topic or the KQ/LO. Play some music, and students need to pass their paper round the class/table. When the music stops, students need to add any extra information to the mind-map in front of them. This could be repeated a few more times and then the sheets are returned to the initial student and stuck in books. The student should now have a mind-map that is formed of various ideas from different students. Additionally, this can be used as a translation/solving exercise. Key information can be passed around the room, and when the music stops, students have a set amount of time to work out what the phrase means or the result of the equation, etc.

- Draw what you hear.

Students must work in pairs and sit back to back. One student has something visual whilst the other student has a whiteboard or piece of paper. Student A must describe the visual to the other student without using the word to actually describe what it is. Student B must listen to what is being said and draw what they hear.

- Ranking.

Students are provided with a group of cards with a range of statements/facts, etc. Students must work in small groups to discuss the importance of each card and rank them accordingly. This then leads to class discussion and debate as to why certain groups have placed cards higher or lower than another group.

- **Text the table.**

    Ask students to place the KQ or a question they have created/wish to ask, based on the topic, on a sheet of paper. In a separate box on the sheet, ask them to write their response. They then "text" this to another student (really, just pass the paper but using the word text gets them enthused!) who places their reply in a different box. Allow them to text at least three students to try to build up a jigsaw answer where different input creates a rounded answer.

- **Spin the paper.**

    Students are placed in groups and given a large sheet of paper on which a scenario/question is written (this could also be an exam question). Students each have a space on the paper to write anything they think will help answer that question. This could be key words or full phrases. After a set amount of time, students then need to spin the paper round so that they have someone else's work in front of them to which they read, evaluate and add to. Students should eventually end up with their original question back in front of them so they can see what improvements have been made.

- **Freeze frame.**

    In groups, students create a still of how they have best depicted the topic/what they think is the most useful part of the topic or, how they have been learning. Students cannot move, but the rest of the class can ask them questions as to why they have chosen these positions.

- **Carousel lessons.**

    These are, by far, my favourite kind of lessons and the ideal way to allow students to find information by working in groups. I have found it best to have three stations that are repeated as six stations can be far too much for students to cope with within one lesson. Each student has a role within the group such as Progress Police or Literacy Leader and must contribute to the group and evidence this in the lesson in order to be rewarded. I have found it best to provide students with an information sheet to fill in as they go round with extension activities available. Also, ensure that before they move to the next station, a pit stop takes place, and a progress check is carried out. The aim of the carousel is that students spend time at different stations to independently obtain a variety of different information. I often have match up cards at one station, a reading activity at another and a speaking activity at station 3. The different stations should permit students to access different skills.

---

Nombre: _____     Target: _____

### Information Sheet - El arte
In your groups, work together to find out the following information!

1) SHAPES. What is the Spanish for:
a) Shapes _____
b) Square _____
c) Triangle _____
d) Circle _____
e) Star _____
f) Rectangle _____

**Challenge UNO:**
Can you find any other shapes in a Spanish dictionary? How about a 6 sided shape? An 8 sided shape?

2) COLOURS. What is the Spanish for:
g) colours _____
h) blue _____
i) white _____
j) red _____
k) green _____
l) pink _____
m) black _____
n) yellow _____
o) orange _____
p) violet _____

**Challenge DOS:**
Can you link the colour red to a monkey in only 6 steps? Be as creative as you like!

3) What does ¿te gusta el arte? mean?
_____

4) ADJECTIVES. What is the Spanish for:
q) boring _____
r) fun _____
s) relaxing _____
t) nice _____
u) interesting _____
v) it is _____
w) Because _____

**Challenge TRES:**
Explain, in your own words, why some adjectives have an "o" on the end but sometimes they have an "a".

Finished? Go and grab a challenge card. Write your answer on this sheet in the box provided to earn dojos/vivos! ¡Buena Suerte!

- Running dictation.

This technique works well when you want students to recall key vocabulary/structures/symbols, etc. Place a prepared text/resource at the front of the room. Then have students run to the front, retain as much information as they possibly can and then run back to their group and tell them what they have seen/remembered. One group member could be the scribe. Then, another group member runs to the front to try to retain as much as they can, and so, it continues until the activity has been completed. A variation of this is to display one text on the whiteboard and display it for a certain amount of time, whilst the class are working in small groups to try to remember as much as they can. When time is up, blank the screen and ask students to write as much as they can remember in their books/on paper or using the table with a washable marker. I also like to extend this by giving them different coloured pens to correct their mistake or, placing a "spend the words" (see incorporating literacy and numeracy) slide on the board and asking them to improve the text, keeping a running total of how much they spend.

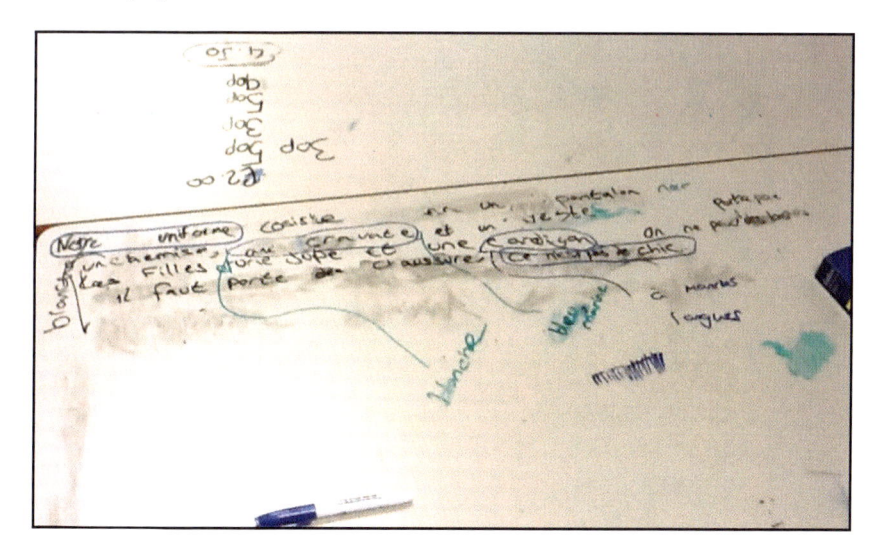

- Information hunt.

Hide key pieces of information around the classroom/corridors for students to find. You could differentiate this by either giving students a task sheet to complete whilst hunting or tell them that they need to find what they believe are the most important factors to retain, in order to meet the LO or answer the KQ.

- **Balloon words.**

This technique is better with smaller groups but is an engaging way to summarise a topic. Students have the aim of building the biggest balloon tower but certain rules are in place, e.g. they have sticky tape but are only allowed two centimetres at a time (get a ruler out and you've incorporated a bit of numeracy!) and can only take one balloon at a time. A student runs to the front to grab a balloon and a whiteboard marker. They need to blow the balloon up and write on it, within the time limit set, criteria that the teacher has called out, e.g. five adjectives or five multiples of seven, etc. Students cannot use anything, but the sticky tape to help support their tower and must only build up balloons if they have the right amount of words on. Then, here comes the fun (but a little scary!) bit…the teacher then circulates the room as they are building towers and pops any balloons that do not match up to the criteria meaning that they have to replace the balloon or start from scratch in rebuilding if the tower is demolished. My year 11s were totally engrossed in this and not only did it consolidate their understanding of the key topic but also stretched their decision-making skills, teamwork, logic and numeracy skills (measuring the tape and the height of the final tower!)

- **Making decisions.**

Give students cards that accompany a text, video or song. Some of the statements should be true whilst others should be false. Students need to study the text or watch the video and work out which statement should be removed as a result of them being false.

- Working co-operatively.

You will need to divide a topic up into sub-topics (4 works best) that require students to study the same materials but from different points of view. The students should work in groups to create a resource summarising any information given and expressing their opinions. After a set amount of time, students should then split up so that there is one member from each sub-topic now working together. They should take it in turns to share information so that they ultimately end up having an overview of all four sub-topics but have done so through peer teaching and questioning.

- Roll up, Roll up!

Turn your classroom into an environment where students go shopping for answers. Divide students into groups and assign various roles such as market trader and shopper. Provide students with resources to read and ask them to summarise it in a resource of their own using only pictures or a set amount of words (not too many as the idea is that you want them to absorb the information, not copy it). Students then use this as a teaching resource. Some members of the group go shopping to other groups whilst one or two stay behind to staff the shop, essentially teaching those who come to visit.

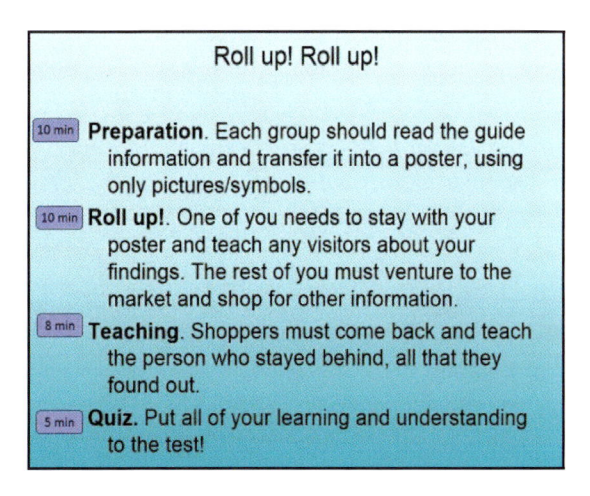

> **Roll up! Roll up!**
>
> [10 min] **Preparation**. Each group should read the guide information and transfer it into a poster, using only pictures/symbols.
>
> [10 min] **Roll up!**. One of you needs to stay with your poster and teach any visitors about your findings. The rest of you must venture to the market and shop for other information.
>
> [8 min] **Teaching**. Shoppers must come back and teach the person who stayed behind, all that they found out.
>
> [5 min] **Quiz**. Put all of your learning and understanding to the test!

- Scenarios.

Make your classroom a world of imagination by setting a scene. When teaching the topic of food and drink, my classroom becomes a make believe French café. Ask students to visualise the scene and ask questions to prompt: "What can you see/hear?" "What food is in front of you?" "What's the atmosphere like?" Give them post-it notes to write their visions on and ask them to stick them around the room based on where it would be found in a real-life situation. Then, ask students to circulate the room, asking questions to one another as to why they have put that or what it means.

Teaching the topic of holidays? Ask students to write a list of what they would take on a scrap piece of paper (in real life, they would not write it neatly in a book so relate this learning to real life! The same way that if you are teaching about a war and trying to get students to imagine they have been recruited, do not get them writing a neat goodbye letter in their books, quickly rip up paper and ask them to jot down their notes on this paper) Give certain items a weight and tell the students that they have a weight limit (quick numeracy link!). Bring in scales or create fake scales and have the students weighing their baggage. Too heavy? They will need to work out what to take out by giving items a rating of importance.

- Props.

Use props where possible to stimulate learning and creativity. The props could be obvious in relation to the topic or use random items to stretch student's imagination. A bag full of random objects is a great way to get them thinking, speaking and writing creatively. If you do not have props yourself or do not have the time to make them, get students into groups and have them design and create something related to the lesson's learning. Use this as an opportunity for them to pitch their ideas to one another, asking for investment, (rewards!) and sparking debate.

- Imagination station.

Sketch a picture on the board or have an image displayed and ask students to name the places. Apart from the obvious: no rude or offensive words, allow students to run with this, using their vivid imaginations. Ask students to come and label the picture with their words. From this, ask questions: "I really like that, why did you call it that?" From this, a story will come, and before you know it, students will be creatively writing. Gather students around the image, ask lots of questions, get lots of answers and then set the task of actually writing it all down. You can bet that students will be far more willing to do this after having this type of discussion than if you were just to set a writing task straight away. Continue to stretch their imagination and creativity by setting the next scene. Tell them that something big/bad/problematic has to happen to the image, e.g. if it is a local café, tell them that a big, popular supermarket wants to buy the plot and that the employees will all lose their jobs. Question them on what they would do and if it is fair. This will then soon lead to persuasive writing and encourage them to protest (in a good way)! Linking lessons to real life scenarios has a real impact on learning and sells the lesson to the students because they can see the value of learning it. Personalising lessons is important, whether it be through a method like this or proving to the students that you are not a robot and letting them find out (suitable) information about you through a topic.

- **It's a mystery.**

Split students into groups and provide them with at least five cards (face down) that have statements about the topic covered during the lesson. For higher ability groups, it might be worthwhile putting in some red herrings! Provide students with a list of questions related to the topic, which should eventually match up to the statements previously given. Students need to match the statements to the questions by speaking only. They cannot show the members of the group the statements and they cannot use the exact phrasing on the sheet.

When carrying out active learning, it is fundamental that students are given roles. You may wish for them to keep the same role every time an active learning task/group task is carried out or you may prefer to assign different roles to different students each time. Some ideas I have used and that have been successful are as follows:

- Progress Police.

These students are in charge of commenting on how the group has moved forward during the lesson. They could evidence this on paper or through a conversation with you. They are also able to create questions/quizzes for other members of their team or other groups to check understanding. I have found that playing a siren sound, is a successful gesture in encouraging the students to stop the task and discuss the steps they have made toward answering the KQ.

- Literacy leader.

These students are responsible for checking any written work and ensuring that punctuation is correct as well as spelling, and they also have the job of finding out the meaning of new words. They also have the chance to peer assess another group, commenting on literacy strengths and weaknesses. These students are always armed with a highlighter and dictionary!

- Super spy.

This role is a popular one amongst students as it entails "stealing" information from other groups. When a signal (I use a whistle or the Pink Panther theme tune) is given, spies can go to another group and can search for information that might also be useful to their group. Tables are not allowed to hide their work, and spies cannot remove the work from the table or write anything down. If they find something they like, they must retain the information and bring it back to their original team.

- Quirky questioner.

At the beginning of the task, students should have a discussion with their team about any questions they wish to ask regarding the task/content of the task (I normally limit each group to two questions). In addition, they are responsible for formulating questions to pose to other groups throughout the task and are also responsible for maintaining the focus of their group.

- **Smart Scribe.**

This role is given to those who are responsible for either writing during written/dictation tasks or, if this is not needed, they are in charge of summarising key points/discussion notes that their group is making during a task. Clarify that they are also required to explain these points and should also note down any rewards their team receives. The student in this role could also be permitted to award rewards (as long as they have a limit) to team members that they think are working well.

---

**Wait Your Turn!**

Students have to work as a class and can only speak when standing. Two students cannot be standing at once so must wait their turn and listen to each other.

# 11. BEHAVIOUR MANAGEMENT

How do you typically start your lessons? Is it with words that acknowledge bad behaviour, e.g. "Sit down", "Get on with your starter activity" and "Put your phone away". Or, is it identifying and praising good behaviour? "Well Done, Tera, you've opened your book and you are doing exactly as I expect." Starting a lesson positively is a great way to maintain good behaviour throughout. Greeting students at the door with a smile and possibly even a compliment (even if it is the class you have been dreading all week!) is the first step towards consistent, good behaviour.

The following techniques have worked for me. Therefore, I hope they will be of some use to you!

- "Sssshers"

    Give the louder students the role of being a "ssssher"! When you raise your hand/count down, have them being the ones quietly reminding the group to shhhhh!

- Trade cards.

    Use these to provide specific targets to students. I use the cut out of a hand with the word TRADE written on it and targets such as: "Avoid calling out", "Complete all class work" and "Volunteer two answers in the lesson". If the students meet these targets by the end of the lesson, they can trade the card for a reward. I do not necessarily give these just to the "naughty" students but quiet students and the middle cohort also.

- Contracts.

Create a contract for a specific student and agree on the targets. Have the student sign this contract and set a date for when they should complete the contract. Agree on the reward for if they do well, e.g. positive phone call/postcard but also let them know what the consequence will be should they fail, e.g. detention/negative phone call. Display the contract where they can see it and should the student start to misbehave in the lesson, give a quick glance at the contract.

- Noise-o-meter.

If you have an iPad/iPhone, there is a free noise-o-meter app available online, which detects the sounds in the room and shows the students when they are too loud. Don't have the app? Draw your own noise-o-meter on the board and draw arrows to represent the noise levels, e.g. silence/whisper/pair-work/too loud. Use warning symbols as a prompt for students to take responsibility for their volume! Set them a limit per lesson, e.g. three warning symbols = class detention.

- Stickers.

Use them on a reward chart, either for individual students or classes. I have two, bottom set Year 8 groups and they are in competition with each other through the use of a sticker chart. I award a certain amount of stickers for progress made, behaviour, questions asked, etc. Stickers can also be used like a loyalty card, e.g. five stickers/stamps = school reward (we use vivos), seven = postcard home, ten = phone call home.

- **Controlling low-level disruption.**

Never try to talk over the students. Stand with your hand in the air until students start copying you and the class becomes quiet. A variation on this would be to start counting whilst your hand is up and however many seconds you have to wait translate into minutes that the students now owe you.

- **Teacher vs. Students.**

Have a visible scoreboard. If the class are too noisy/disruptive, give yourself a point. However, every time they are quiet and on-task, reward them with a point. If you win, the class have to face the consequence set. This could be a detention or extra homework. However, if they win, you will have to find a suitable reward for the class that could be stickers, points, a game next lesson or a week off of homework!

- **Don't lose your temper!**

However much a class is annoying you, try to remain calm and do not raise your voice. Use please and thank you at the end of your requests, e.g. "Tony, could you sit down, please?"

- **Keep them challenged.**

Some students often cause trouble because they are bored. Ensure that you have a range of extension/thinking activities available to maintain their focus.

- **Read my lips.**

To settle a rowdy class or to get them back after a more lively activity, silently mouth instructions and get them to lip read. Ask for a translator or get them writing your requirements on a whiteboard.

- **5, 4, 3 (2, 1)**

To get silence without raising your voice, count from 5-3 aloud, asking the students to count with you. Then, you and the students count 2-1 silently in your heads meaning that you have silence ready for issuing the next task/reviewing the previous one.

- Individual behaviour plan.

These are very much like the trade cards and the contract, but the students have them stuck in the front of their books. Students must stick to these targets over a sequence of lessons and should be rewarded with a sticker/stamp every time they achieve each target. Agree on a number of stickers to receive a bigger reward such as a phone call/postcard home.

- Warning cones/post-it notes for non-verbal gestures.

Use a post-it/warning cone (can be bought in the 99p shop) and place on the desk of the student who is disrupting. This helps you avoid raising your voice, and the student can visually see that they need to do something to improve their behaviour. An alternative to this is to write targets on the table in washable pen so that they are visible to the student throughout the lesson.

## 12. PRAISE AND REWARDS

- **Consider the age.**

Is something you give to a Year 7 also appropriate for a Year 11? Have a range of rewards that will suit all ages and learners.

- **Consistency.**

Consistency is key, but do not "over-reward". Too many rewards or praising, just for the sake of praising, loses its value.

Parents/carers need to hear the praise too as do Year Leaders and Form Tutors!

- **Know your students.**

You need to know what they will work hard for. Not all students appreciate being praised in front of the whole class whilst others do.

Make sure they know what you are praising/rewarding them for. Praise needs to be genuine, sincere and specific.

- **Use proximity praise.**

Instead of focusing on the child who is disengaged, praise those who are attending to the task and completing their work. (Catch someone being good!)

- Remember.

Do not forget to reward if you have said you will! Students remember everything that we do not really need them to!

Think about your tone of voice when praising. Make sure you really are genuine and ensure that different actions have different rewards, e.g. someone coming in and sitting down ready to work might just be verbal praise, as it is what they are expected to do. However, a student who goes beyond your expectations with class work or feedback might deserve something more.

Rewards do not have to be of a monetary value. In fact, I have found the most effective rewards to be those of warmth and positivity. Most students want nothing more than a phone call home to share recognition of their good work, however this cannot be used all of the time so, some other ideas are as follows:

- The good old-fashioned sticker!

This could be taken further by a certain amount of stickers resulting in a phone call home or a postcard home. My Year 10s and 11s absolutely love collecting stickers on the front cover of their books and I reward the student with the most stickers at the end of each term with a small prize to make this collecting worthwhile.

- Star of the week/reward certificates.

Display them in the corridor or send them home.

- Wristbands.

Wristbands are a great way of rewarding and giving praise. The wristbands can be used to write exactly how the student has done well, and they love wearing them and showing them off around school. Furthermore, aside from a reward, the wristbands are an excellent way to set targets for behaviour management. Having them around their wrist means that students have no excuse for forgetting them. Alternatively, the wristbands can be used as a revision tool where students write key words/spellings on them, which need to be learned.

- Raffle.

Raffle tickets can be given for good behaviour, excellent work, exemplary homework or improvements in attitude or behaviour. These can be placed in a jar and either called at the end of the lesson or the end of a term/half term with a reward as a result.

- Points system/League table.

Points allocated for certain things, e.g. organised = 5 points, excellent classwork = 10 points, etc. Then have a total number of points that equate to a prize. Students can decide to "cash" them in when/if they would like. The league table could be done within individual classes or across year groups to promote extended competition.

- Verbal Contribution Chip.

I created these in my first year of teaching and still use them now. I used a picture of a casino chip on a sticker and awarded them every time a student participated verbally within the lesson. This could be to ask, answer or add to a question. The students can then decide to collect them up by banking them in their book or spend them on prizes, e.g. 10 chips = a pencil, 20 chips = star of the week, 30 chips = a week off of homework.

- **Class Dojo.**

Classdojo.com is a great alternative to offer alongside other rewards. Each student is assigned a monster, and they can receive points for a variety of efforts. If you have an iPad/iPhone, you can project the app onto the whiteboard/smart board and students can see points being added immediately. This website allows you to generate reports and certificates, which can be handed to the students.

- **Secret Student.**

At the start of the lesson, inform the class that someone in the room is going to be picked at random to be the lesson's Secret Student. Once this has been identified, as students are set on a task, whisper a signal word to the secret student, tap the chair, or create some kind of signal to indicate that they are the chosen one! It is important that no other student finds out about this secret. Tell the class that as long as this student remains on task and completes all work, the whole class will receive a reward.

- **Display their work.**

A simple, yet very effective form of praise is to display their work in the classroom. (I display only the very best work on clipboards, on the wall. Students know this so strive to get their work on the Wall of Fame!) Take a photo of it on the wall and send it home with a praise letter!

- Virtual money.

Give virtual money, which students can save or spend during the lesson. I give them an opportunity to spend the money by "selling" things and students can decide to spend their own money or group together with a friend if they do not quite have enough. They can buy a game or can spend their money on an answer/clue to a question. However, I also take money away. Should a student forget a pen, they need to spend virtual money on buying one. If they have no money, I ask them to swap something, e.g. phone, planner or bag that they will get back once my pen is returned. They can also lose money through lack of homework, poor class work or unacceptable behaviour. The element of money teaches them the value of it and also incorporates numeracy by getting them to add totals and change required.

**BANK OF MISS. SARGENT**

£100

EXCELLENT CLASSWORK / HOMEWORK ☐    GREAT GROUP WORK ☐

BRILLIANT BEHAVIOUR ☐                OUTSTANDING PROGRESS ☐

PERFECT PARTICIPATION ☐              AMAZING ATTITUDE ☐

- Scratch cards.

Scratch cards can be used as a reward for excellent classwork and homework, or for answering questions in the lesson. They take some time to set up, but the students **LOVE** them. Provide a jackpot at the bottom of the card and give them three things to match under the sticker, e.g. "Match 3 connectives/match 3 multiples of 7/ find 3 field events or create a sentence with the words to win the jackpot". I have also used these in marking, and students have had to scratch the sticker to find a secret word that they have to get into the lesson as many times as possible or to see their EBI. If you do not have the time to create them, you could set the students a task of creating a card, using a question they have formulated based on their learning.

- King/Queen for the lesson.

I purchased an inflatable crown from a supermarket, and it has proven to be one of the best forms of motivation for students! They get to wear the crown for a variety of reasons; 1) if they answer a question/series of questions correctly (crown passes to next student who gets a question correct, making the current crown holder eager to keep hold of it!) 2) awarding the crown to the most impressive worker/best participator/best homework/best question, etc. at the end of the lesson so they get to wear it for the duration of the next class. I often give them the title of King or Queen Expert and students can ask the crown wearer for advice on completing work.

# 13. LEARNING ENVIRONMENT

Your classroom should stimulate the students and have interactive displays to engage them and support them in their work.

Before displaying something, THINK. How will this help the students? Additionally, your classroom should become whatever you want it to be based on the topic your teaching. Teaching about habitats? Make it into a pretend beach or forest. This does not mean you bringing in sand and fake trees but expanding the student's imagination.

Make your room, a room that inspires.

Desk arrangement is important. Different arrangements of desks encourage different types of working skills. Desks in groups, facing each other can help stimulate student discussion while desks in single or double rows are good for demonstrations and independent work. Furthermore, desks in "work stations" are suited to students who have developed skills allowing them to work together and individually.

Alongside desk arrangement, displays are important in aiding learning and student's work should be displayed where possible.

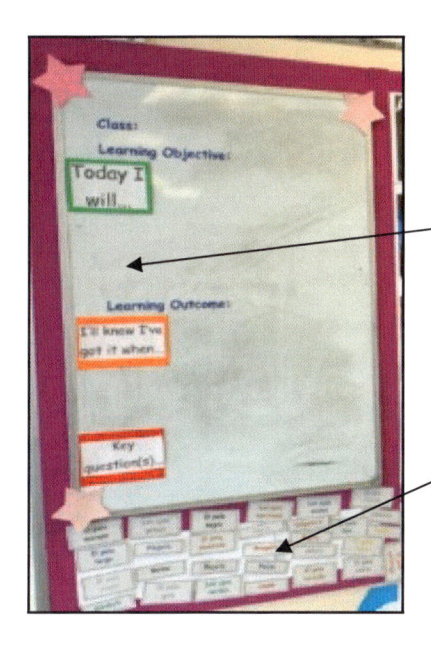

Have a dedicated area to display the KQ/LO.

Also try to incorporate removable key words where possible to encourage students to include them in their work by placing them on their desk or asking the TA to test their understanding of topical words.

Set up a permanent challenge desk and help desk and establish a routine whereby students are able to use these independently.

- Use chalk pens to display key information on windows.
- Bunting can be used as a way to celebrate students by placing their names and achievements on flags.

Use wall space effectively, dividing it between displays of student's work and key words that occur across a number of topics. Students will get used to using these displays regularly, and you are less likely to have to remind them to use connectives, openers, range of vocabulary, etc. because they are readily available to them.

Display student's work in a creative way to encourage them to complete their own work in a similar manner. Ensure that all displayed work has been marked and use as examples to other students/classes.

**Word of the week:** Pamplemousse

**Phrase of the week:** Bonne chance!

**Verb of the week:** Faire

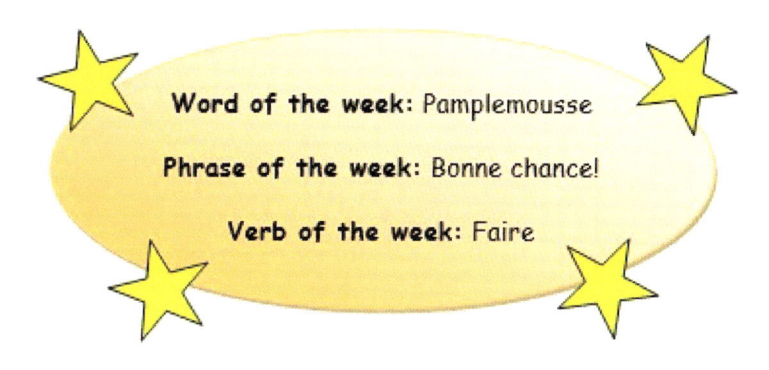

Have a word/phrase/verb of the week. The challenge for students is to include these accurately in their work in order for a reward.

Have a dedicated area to promote literacy and numeracy and make them interactive. You could use lolly sticks in pockets/envelopes that students can take to their desks and incorporate in their work. You could also set them challenges by having to include three lolly stick words in their work.

Ensure that levels/grade criteria are displayed in the room so that students can refer to them whilst completing work. As I mentioned in the AfL section, students cannot be expected to produce what is needed to achieve levels/grades if they do not know how!

Where possible use acronyms/logos to display key components of what is expected in the work. I am sure you have heard of SPaG, so try to develop something similar related to your subject/topic. Have examples so that students have a starting point.

Ensure that your displays are useful and help students to be successful. If I say, "Use star words", students know to look to the wall where I have a range of connectives in star shapes or, "Use cupboard words" means they instantly head to the back cupboards where they have a variety of key vocabulary.

Use all areas of your classroom to display work/resources for support to ensure that students have model work as examples and are stimulated by what is around them. The following posters can be found on the ceiling of my classroom and are a regular talking point when we study the topic of town/shops.

99

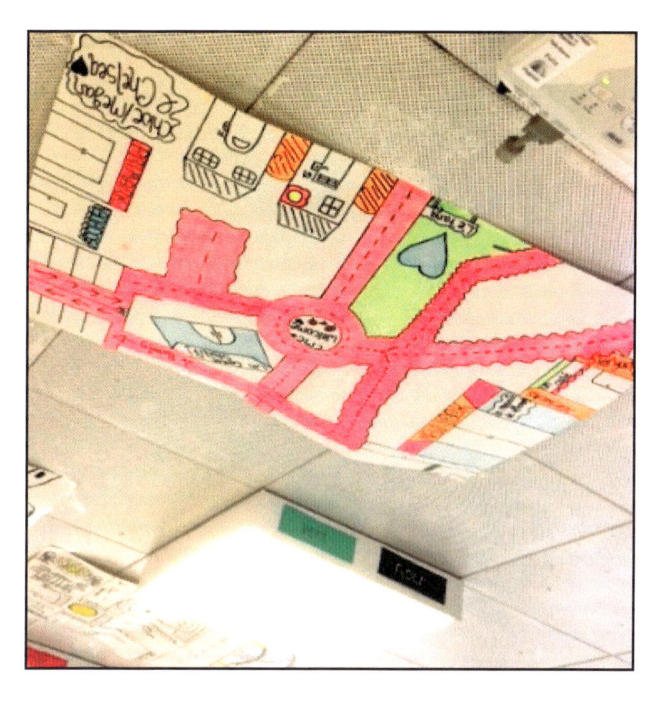

# 14. USE OF THE TEACHING ASSISTANT

**Effective use of the Teaching Assistant must cater for students in your class. This does not just mean the top and bottom abilities but all cohorts.**

**You have a duty to let your TA know, in advance, what will be covered in the lesson and how you would like to deploy them. Set up an agreement with the TA to decide on how you would like them to work in the classroom.**

Some ideas are as follows:

- Tandem teach.

Pre-determine a group in which you would like the TA to work with. Whilst you are teaching the rest of the class, the TA is teaching a smaller group. This could be in order to stretch them, therefore, using differentiated resources/explanations or, it could be to support a weaker cohort.

- Directed questioning

Provide the TA with a generic list of questions that they could ask students at points in the lesson questions could include:

**1.** Can you give me one key word you have learnt today? Could you use it in a sentence?

**2.** In your opinion, what is the most important thing you have learnt today?

**3.** Can you teach me something you have looked at in the lesson today?

**4.** Can you explain how you have been learning today?

**5.** Would you change the lesson? How?

**6.** How will this help you for your next lesson?

**7.** Imagine an alien has walked in the room. Can you explain what you have learned?

**8.** Can you create a question to ask me about the lesson?

**9.** What have been your strengths and weaknesses of this lesson?

**10.** What skills have you used during this lesson?

- Challenges.

Alongside generic questioning, provide the TA with some challenges that they could distribute to students who need stretching. These could include:

- Create a comic strip to show what and how you have learned today.

- Write a set of 10 questions to test me, or a partner, on today's lesson.

- Race me to find five words linked to the KQ, using a dictionary.

- Draw a picture showing what you have learnt today.

- Create a starter activity for the next lesson to test me.

- Re-wording.

The TA should be able to address the class if they see that a common misconception is occurring. The TA could use this opportunity to help re-word the task or ask the teacher to re-teach the topic/help the teacher re-teach in a different way.

- Involving the TA in games.

Use the TA to lead a group/half of the class during a game/plenary. A popular game among my classes is as follows:

- Divide the class in half and teacher and TA lead a team each.

- Using a ball for each team, decide on which student will start, but the TA/ teacher must finish.

- Students must state something that has been learnt during the lesson and pass the ball to the next person. The TA/teacher is in charge of listening for words said, and any repeated words/incorrect words means that the ball must be taken back to the start.

- The competitive element of this task engages the students and involves the TA in the task and increases their recognition in the classroom.

- Modelling answers.

Use the TA as a means to model expectations and examples. The TA could also ask leading questions during pit stops to enhance the understanding of students on a specific topic, e.g. if you have just covered vocabulary for shops, the TA could ask the class: "What's a bakery, in Spanish?"

- Correcting work.

Providing the TA with a green pen is a quick and easy way to assist in marking and student understanding. The TA can circulate the room, providing advice and feedback where necessary.

- **Non-verbal signals.**

Remember, a TA is not there to control the class. Therefore, the teacher and the TA should agree on a non-verbal signal that the TA gives to a student to help maintain focus and behaviour.

- **Mini-whiteboards.**

A mini-whiteboard is an essential tool for a TA, provide one each lesson for your TA as a means to write down keywords for specific students or as a way to note rewards. The key words could be used as a prompt for students who struggle with starting work, or more challenging words could be used to stretch the more able. Additionally, the TA could use this as a gap fill exercise for students.

- **Praise.**

Give the TA a set of stickers or batch of postcards to award to the students on the spot in lessons. This helps students build a rapport with the TA.

- **Feedback.**

As a teacher, having a TA in the class is the best means of acquiring feedback on students or lessons. Take the time to catch 5 minutes with the TA after a lesson to have a conversation about who did well/might need extra help in follow-up lessons.

- **Small groups.**

Send pairs or small groups to the TA to consolidate learning. This could involve a match up task or a sentence building task. The students should race against each other, and the TA should reward those who do well. My TA has a league table for who has done well each time we carry out an activity like this, and she will reward the winner with a prize at the end of each half term.

- Beat the TA!

Have an activity for individual students whereby they race the TA to find certain words related to a topic.

- Mistake making.

Either you or the TA summarises the learning at a key point in the lesson but makes a purposeful mistake. You or the TA should then flag this up: "Erm, Miss, I don't quite understand as that's not what you said earlier…" Then, ask the students if they can help (a very powerful thing is asking students for their help) to correct it by identifying the mistake and re-explaining. A lot of successful use of the TA comes from modelling and role play.

It is imperative that you either discuss in person or email a plan to the TA for **EACH** lesson, in advance of it taking place.

Remember, a TA isn't a mind-reader and needs to know how you want them to work during the lesson. They will always need time to process your plans and prepare anything required for it. Imagine, being taken for a cover lesson at the last minute and having no guidelines on what to do!

Therefore, in my emails, I include vocabulary needed for the lesson, any questions they could ask and then how I would like them to specifically work, whether that be with an individual, a group or pairs. The TA can see this in advance and brings it to the lesson with them. My TAs are great and will often annotate the email after the lesson to let me know what worked/what did not or how they think the lesson should progress/be modified in order to be more successful in aiding learner's understanding.

In addition to this short-term plan, it is worthwhile creating a long-term plan with your TA that includes strategies that you would like them to use on a regular basis with specific students and the whole class. Furthermore, on this plan, you could include a break-down of the SOW so that they can see what is coming up and what they need to prepare for.

A TA is an invaluable resource in the classroom so treat them well! They are the eyes in the back of your head that you always tell the students you have!

**Subject:** Support for Year 8

Morning,

**Students requiring support-**
Student XXX (Statement)Anger issues but responds well to praise. Needs firm boundaries and consequences. Please give non-verbal signals to keep behaviour/focus on track and reward with stickers and postcard if appropriate.
Student ZZZ- (Statement) Responds really well to praise but needs constant reminders to be on task and challenges set. Please encourage xxx to start the same time as everyone else and break each task down in to manageable chunks using the laminated sheet. Please leave xxx for the first 10 minutes of the lesson, allowing him to process information using the laminated sheet. Please don't make him feel like you are only helping him.

**Support for whole class-**
If you see particularly good work or improvements, please award vivos/dojos or for exceptional work, please write a postcard with a short message and hand to the student in the class, signing the postcard.
Please ask me a question in front of the class if you feel that the whole class may need something re-wording.
Please could you ask a question to the class during pit-stop? This could be a translation or a spelling test on a key word.

**Vocab required-** (list from last week but they are now putting sentences together!)
Please could you take pairs, with whiteboards and test them on the following sentences. Award most accurate/fastest student with a point for the league table. Ask them to explain why they've written that answer.

1) I hate horror films because they are boring- **odio las peliculas de terror porque son aburridas**
2) I love comedies because they are funny- **me encantan las comedias porque son graciosas**
3) I like westerns because they are interesting- **Me gustan las peliculas del Oeste porque son interesantes**
4) I like the news because it is important- **Me gusta el telediario porque es interesante**
5) I don't like romantic films because they are silly- **no me gustan las peliculas de amor porque son tontas**

**Aim of the lesson-** Student ZZZ to work independently with no more than one reminder about the task. All students to agree at least 2 adjectives correctly! **Thank you in advance!**

105

# 15. GAMES

Games are a fundamental part of learning. That is not to say that you simply crack open the Monopoly board, but a well thought out game adds value to learning and makes what can often be difficult topics, accessible.

> **TIP:** When playing games that involve giving an answer, give students buzzer sounds or animal noises. My Year 11 class can often be heard mooing, meowing, woofing and hissing.
> It definitely minimises the amount of blurting out
> the answer as they make their noise first!

- Pass the parcel.

    - Revises key words/structures/formula;

    - Provides an opportunity for students to ask each other questions;

    - Promotes jig-sawing if answers can be built on;

- Explains a problem...

**HOW DOES IT WORK?**

Play music and pass the box/bag/envelope round the room. When you stop the music, the student with the box opens it and picks one folded paper at random then completes the task/question. To avoid half the class sitting out whilst the parcel is passed round the other side of the room, have two or three parcels being passed at once.

**Variation 1:** Colour coded pass the parcel with differentiated questions. Easier questions in a green box, medium in amber and difficult in red. You could have different rewards tied to each question and give the students the opportunity to swap.

**Variation 2:** All too often, students pass the box around at lightning speed because they are worried about it landing on them. Why not have it so that when the music stops, whoever has the box, gets to nominate someone to answer a question?

**Variation 3:** Roulette-pass the parcel. Amongst the questions in the container, also place some nasty forfeits or some nice treats, e.g. extra homework, sticker, mime your learning or explain your learning in the style of Miley Cyrus.

- **Musical Chairs.**

Not just for a children's party! This is better played before a free period, lunch or period 5 due to the setting up and clearing away that it requires.

Move the tables out of the way. Make a large circle with one less chair than the number of students in your group. Play music with students moving around, and when you stop the music, they need to sit down. Whoever did not get a chair has to do the chosen task/answer the set question. Get it right, and they get to stay in. Incorrect? They lose their place in the game and should be given a task to either improve their understanding on the point they have wrong or a separate task needs to be given.

- **Guess what I'm thinking.**

Give each student a key word related to the topic of the lesson or ask them to think of their own. Students should work in pairs and use questioning to get information out of each other until they guess correctly what the other one is thinking. However, they can only answer with yes or no.

- Is it a country?
- Is it in Europe?
- Do they speak French?

- **Secret Spy.**

This is a great way to help students learn sequences or train memory skills through repetition.

Keywords/expressions/symbols/number sequences are on the board in a list. One student, who is now known as the detective, is sent out of the room. One student in the room is the secret spy and provides the signal to the teacher. This could be a wink, a tap of a pen or a flick of the hair. The detective is then brought back to the room. The whole class then continuously repeats the item at the top of the list until the teacher is given the signal by the secret spy, meaning that the class move on to repeating the next item in the sequence. The detective has three goes at spotting the secret spy and can circulate the room if need be. A great trick with this is to use the TA in your room if you have one. With them giving the signal, the detectives are stumped every time!

- **Ready, Steady... Draw!**

The class is divided into two teams. One member from each team comes to the whiteboard, and the teacher secretly shows them a key word/phrase. The two students at the front then have to draw or write the keyword behind their backs, on the whiteboard, without looking. After a set time limit, the teacher asks the two at the front to move away from the board, and the teams have to try to guess the given word.

The concentration on their faces is priceless as they face the front with their hands behinds their back, tongues hanging out, trying to draw the keyword!

If drawing behind the back is too difficult for the words you are covering, you can vary it by allowing them to look at the board but stick to only drawing and allow no words. I often do it this way if I want the students to recognise a phrase rather than just a word.

- Snowball fight!

Have students line up in two teams with a board pen. They must run to the board, write something they have learned today/answer to a question/keyword then pass the pen and run to the back of the queue. To provide challenge, ask students to write words in alphabetical order or ask them to sequence the words so that they make sense. Alternatively, ask them to make a sentence from the key words or have teams swap places and correct any mistakes/provide a definition to the key word.

With languages, this works really well in consolidating the grammar by asking students to sequence pronouns and verbs.

Winning team is the team who has the first person back to the front and no repetition on the board.

- Draw what you know.

Grab student's attention by drawing something on the board related to the lesson and asking them to guess what it is. As soon as a student guesses correctly, ask them to add something they think could also be related to this idea, through drawing (intervene by giving a key word if they appear stuck!). This then continues until a bigger picture has been built on the board, representing the topic of the lesson.

Students also like to do this in teams/pairs by drawing on the tables with a whiteboard pen. They translate key words/phrases from the lesson into pictures and partners have to guess what it is. Or, rather than a partner guess, the partner then adds something else to the picture and another pair guesses the key word(s)/phrase.

I recently carried this out with the topic of jobs and students loved it. Drawing their understanding rather than writing is a welcome change to most of them.

- Beat the Teacher.

They get **VERY** excited with this one, as they believe they can grab a baseball bat and start whacking you! However, fortunately, this game is not quite like that! Instead, it involves the teacher displaying key images/symbols on the board related to the lesson. The teacher then points to one and says what it is, either correctly or incorrectly. If correct, all students must repeat the phrase out loud. However, if the teacher has pointed to the image/symbol but said it incorrectly, the students must stay absolutely silent, not even a whisper!

Being very competitive, I like to make this interesting by putting something on the line such as homework or reduced game time. If the students win, they are rewarded, but if you win, they have to stick to their side of the bargain! Be warned, if using this technique, you will meet some strong negotiators!

- Forbidden words.

Teacher asks for a volunteer to come to the front with their back to the board. A key word is displayed, which the remaining students must describe without using any of the other given words, e.g. "Describe the word **Twilight** without using, boring, waste of time, I know it all already, ugh!, I could be planning/marking right now!!" A variation of this is to ask students to draw what is being described (again, without using any obvious words) and then match their drawing to the original, e.g. "Draw a straight line at xx degrees, then add…"

- **Stand Up/Sit Down.**

Want students to learn a sequence or pattern? Then, this game works a treat. After having taught the content of the lesson, tell students that they need to recall the sequence, in order by standing up and saying part one of it. Another student then needs to stand up and say part two. The third student says part three and so on. If two students stand up at once and say the same thing, all must sit down, and the sequence has to start from the beginning. This develops their listening and team working skills.

- **Sweet Shop.**

Using a bag of sweets where sweets have different shapes/colours is a way of questioning, summarising and assessing but students just see it as an opportunity to act like they have never seen a sweet before in their life and will do anything for one! I often use Skittles or M&Ms because of the colour variety. On the board, I place a question/task to each colour of sweet. Students then come, pick a sweet from the bag, and have to do the task/answer the question related to the colour. Alternatively, I place sweets on student's tables at the start, again with certain criteria matching each sweet. Students cannot touch/eat/dribble over the sweet until they have included that particular element in their work, e.g. green skittle = use a superlative, red skittle = use at least two connectives and so on.

- **What's your word?**

This works by giving students a key word at the very start of the lesson that will be included within the lesson at some point. Teach as normal and as soon as students hear their word, they need to stand up and say how it has been included within the lesson. This engages students throughout and improves listening skills, as they are intent on finding their word. Reward them when they do but so that they do not lose interest, tell them that it could come up again. If they get to the end of the lesson without having stood up, provide a consequence for not spotting their word.

A variation on this is to not provide students with the keywords yourself but rather, get them to infer what words are likely to come up by placing a picture on the board or simply telling them the topic of the lesson. If you are studying a song, for example, tell them the theme of the song or when it was written or a very brief story behind it. They could come up with words like love, together, unite, etc. Toward the end of the lesson, after teaching more content, play the song and ask them to stand if they hear their word, rewarding as appropriate.

- **Mystery Word.**

Give each student or, selected students, a different, secret word (related to the topic) that they should aim to get in the lesson as many times as possible, without other students noticing. If students are successful, they should be rewarded but if another student notices the mystery word of another, they are rewarded.

- **Puppets/Masks.**

Not so much of a game (although students see it as one) but a method to boost confidence in students when speaking aloud. Using these as a decoy for getting students to share ideas or carry out role-play is an effective method and they are more likely to participate if they believe others are looking at the puppet/mask rather than them.

- **Beach Ball.**

Definitely not suitable for those who do not like noise! Invest in a large inflatable ball that can be written on with marker pen. Using the pen, write question stems or, for a change in questions from lesson to lesson, use post-it notes/labels. Play some music and get students to throw the ball around the classroom. Being a light, inflatable, it does not cause any damage and goes far with a light tap. When the music stops, ask the student who has the ball to answer the question in which their right thumb/middle left finger/right pinky is on.

- **Not saved by the bell (buzzer!)**

(You will need a timer for this but set at different times for each round, e.g. 20 seconds, 50 seconds, 1 minute 20 seconds etc.) Students work in pairs and join with another pair. Two of the pair are "describers" and the other two are "guessers". The describers are given a card with a list of 10 key words/phrases from the lesson/topic. Describer 1 starts by describing the word to their guesser without using the word on the card or gestures. The describer must guess what the word is and as soon as they do, the card is passed to describer 2 who describes the next word in the list to their guesser and so it continues. Whenever the buzzer sounds, the describer with the card in their hand loses a point.

- **Strip Bingo.**

Never fear, no clothes are removed!! Provide students with a piece of paper and ask them to list (must leave enough room between each word to rip a strip) a set amount of key words from the lesson. Teacher calls out first key words (just like normal bingo), and if the student has it, they can rip it off and place it to one side. However, the catch is, is that they can only rip it off if it is at the top or bottom of their page. If it is not, they need to wait until that key word comes round again. The winner is the student who has no words left.

- **Heads Down, Thumbs Up.**

Students introduced this game to me but it had no learning element to it whatsoever, therefore we modified it slightly and use it as follows…4 students are picked to come to the front and the remaining students have to pick 4 main key words from the lesson and assign them to the students. These can be written on the board and students must stand under their respective key word. The remainder of the class put their heads down on the desk, eyes closed, but thumbs sticking up. The four chosen students circulate the class in silence, tapping the thumb of one student each. As soon as all four have picked someone, they come back to the board and stand under their key word. The remainder of the class now stand up if they were picked (there should only be the same amount standing, as the amount of "pickers") and must guess who picked them. They have to say the key word, which is related to the person, but no answers regarding if they are right are given until all have guessed. If students have guessed correctly, they have to give a definition of the key word or provide an example using it in order to swap places.

- **Place Your Bets!**

Give students a set amount of points and ask them to bet a certain amount on the answer to each question. If they get it right, they double their stake but if they get it wrong, they lose their stake. Simple as that!

- **Speed Dating.**

Set your classroom up with two rows of chairs facing each other. Ask students to devise a question based on the learning/general topic and have them ask their potential dating partner that question. Only allow students a short amount of time at each "date", but long enough so that they can ask, answer or teach (if the answer is not known) the question/answer. After a set time, ask the students to move to the next date and repeat the process. At the end of the game, ask students to vote for who they would like to go on a "date" with based on the question asked/answer given or teaching implemented.

- **Silly Sentences.**

Place students into groups of 5 or 6 and place guidelines on the board about what you expect the final outcome to look like. For example, if I were teaching the topic of school subjects, I would place bullet points on the board such as:

- Opinion
- School subject
- Connective
- Opinion

- School subject

- Reason

Student one then writes a phrase/word based on bullet point one, folds their answer over and passes to student two. Student two then writes something based on bullet point two (without looking at what student one has written) and folds their answer over, passing it to student three. This then continues until all students have written something. They can then unfold the paper and read their sentence. Students assess whether their sentences make sense or not and if not, how could they improve them?

This could also be done to summarise learning at the end of a lesson with students reflecting on progress/assessing their learning.

# 16. ENDING THE LESSON — PLENARY TIME

As teachers, we often leave insufficient time for the plenary, however it should not simply be a rushed activity, an activity led or carried out by the teacher or a tidying away exercise, so ensure that you leave at least 10 minutes for an effective plenary.

The plenary should be:

- An opportunity to summarise, reflect and assess learning whilst informing planning for follow-up lessons.

- An opportunity to reflect back on the lesson objectives/key question and draw out learning from students.

- A technique to help students make links in their learning and identify how they have learnt not just what they have learnt.

- An opportunity for students to articulate or show you what has been absorbed.

- As important as the starter.

A quick "go-to" plenary, which requires minimal preparation, is to use learning questions and ask students to complete a journal at the end of the lesson. These learning questions could be displayed on the board or given in the form of plenary dice and while you can vary the way in which you use them (letting star student of the lesson pick the question stem or rolling a die and picking one that relates to a number), they should be standard, routine practice in your classroom.

Some examples of question stems or learning statements are:

1. Today, I have learnt that…

2. The main skill I have been using today is…

3. I can link today's lesson to…

4. The task I enjoyed most/which most helped me was…

5. The most difficult part of the lesson was…

6. I can now say/explain…

7. I overcame a problem today by…

8. The following sentence summarises my learning…

9. If I taught today's lesson, I would change…

10. I already knew…so this helped me in today's lesson by…

11. Can you create a question to challenge someone else in the class? (Allow students to pose these questions to a student of their choice. I carry it out so that if the partner knows the answers, they get the reward. If not, the questioner gets the point but only if they teach us how to get the correct answer).

12. If you were to teach this topic to a family member/friend/alien, how would you do it?

13. Name a phrase/keyword that you have used today and last lesson.

14. What new skills have you learnt?

15. Speak to your partner about their learning today. Find out three things they have learnt and how.

16. What has been your favourite word from the lesson and why?

17. Think of three things you have learned today, turn and share with a partner. Turn the other way and share with a new partner.

However, a plenary does not have to be "right folks, sit in your seats and write me a learning journal". A plenary can be an active part of the lesson.

- **Hot seating.**

Use this technique to call on an expert or a character from the lesson. Ask the rest of the class to think of a question to pose to this student who must answer with as little hesitation as possible.

- **Still images.**

Ask students to summarise their learning through a freeze frame. Ask the remaining students to decipher the freeze frame.

- **Prepare a quiz/activity.**

Either individually or in pairs/small groups, ask students to create a game or quiz to use as a starter activity next lesson (to ensure that all groups get their game seen, you could carry out a carousel style activity where groups move round the class, trialling the different activities) or task to replace one that you carried out in the lesson or that is in the textbook.

- **Count your confidence.**

Ask students to draw a line or an arrow along the top of their page in their book. At intervals in the lesson, as well as at the end, ask students to mark how confident they feel at each stage. Ask students to put a mark on the confidence line when prompted, labelling each stage of the lesson with a number or symbol (this will need a key at the side, e.g. star = starter, smiley face = pit stop one, etc.) Ensure that students annotate their symbols/marks/numbers to show why they feel that particular level of confidence.

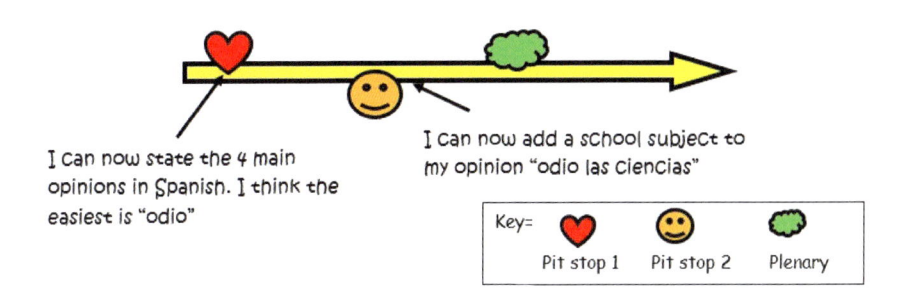

I can now state the 4 main opinions in Spanish. I think the easiest is "odio"

I can now add a school subject to my opinion "odio las ciencias"

Key= ♥ ☺ 🌳
    Pit stop 1  Pit stop 2  Plenary

- **Twitter/Facebook status.**

Ask students to summarise their learning in a status update or, if using the Twitter strategy, give them a specific amount of characters in which they need to comment on their learning. Use a space in your classroom for them to place these on their way out and use them to address any misconceptions in a starter activity in the follow up lesson.

- **You shall not pass (without a ticket!)**

Provide students with a post-it note and use it as their ticket to leave your lesson. They can only exit if they hand in a note that summarises their learning. Keep it simple by asking only two questions such as "What have you learnt today?" and "Which part of the lesson, if any, would you like more help with?"

- **Learning Triangle.**

Use the shape of a triangle to get students reflecting on their learning.

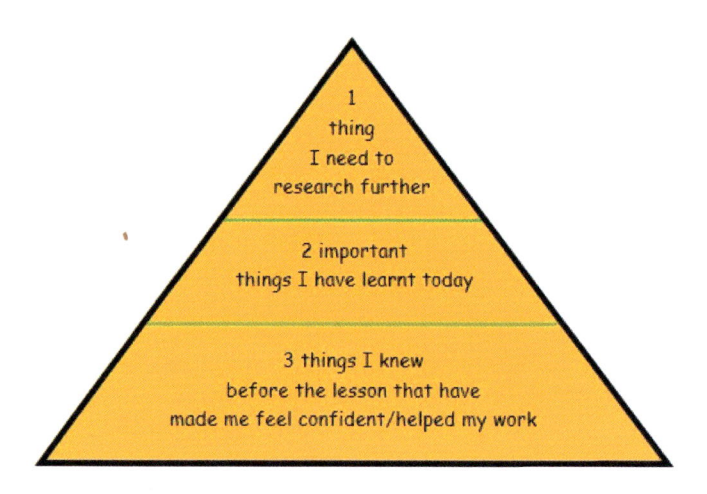

```
        1
      thing
    I need to
  research further

    2 important
  things I have learnt today

      3 things I knew
    before the lesson that have
  made me feel confident/helped my work
```

- **Sentence, word, most important.**

Ask students to summarise their learning in a set number of phrases. Then, ask them to simplify this to a set number of words. Finally, get them to condense all of this to one, key word that they consider the most important from the lesson.

- **Exact Words/Letters.**

Ask students to summarise their learning in an exact amount of words. They cannot have any more or any less than the limit you set. Alternatively, give students a letter or series of letters in which they must sum up the lesson.

- **Guilty/Not Guilty?**

Ask students to provide "evidence" that they have been learning this lesson. They need to provide enough evidence (this could be through answering a series of questions or a whiteboard activity of answering the KQ) to avoid being sent to jail due to lack of learning. I often draw a prison cell on the side of the board and place their names in there if they do not meet the requirements and they face a consequence such as extra research/homework in order to improve their understanding.

- Extend My Sentence/Guess My Sentence.

Provide students with a sentence starter related to the lesson objective or key question and ask them to extend it based on what they have learnt in the lesson. If you have a class requiring support, place some key words on the board that they should endeavour to use within the summary. With Guess My Sentence, ask students to write a phrase, which they think, defines the most important part of their learning. You also do this at the same time on a mini whiteboard (or have one prepared if you prefer). Once the task is completed, turn your whiteboard round and ask students to see if their sentence matches yours, (it is unlikely it will be an exact match so allow some scope here!) rewarding those with a match/close match.

- I Predict a Plenary.

Tell students how the plenary will go at the start of the lesson by giving them a task, e.g. "You'll be a news reporter at the end of the lesson, reporting on your learning, make sure you make key notes as you go through the lesson ready to present the breaking news!" Alternatively, place questions on the board at the start of the lesson, which will be asked during the plenary, encouraging students to think about them in advance.

- Code-Cracker.

Place a code on the board for students to crack in order to find the most important word from today's lesson.

- Time Limit.

Set a timer or play a song and ask students to sum up their learning from the lesson within that time. They either could write as many key words as possible or sentences or even draw their understanding.

- Get Creative!

Ask students to create a mnemonic that helps them remember the meaning of a word within the lesson. An alternative to this is to ask students to create a dictionary definition of their own to describe a word or even create a brand new word to describe how they have learnt or a skill.

- **Mind Reader.**

Based on today's lesson, ask students to predict where the learning will go next. What will we be looking at next lesson? Can you predict a key word that will be in the next lesson?

- **Yes/No?**

Students to respond to your questions WITHOUT using yes or no. This develops their thinking skills as they have to re-word answers/extend answers.

- **Headlines/Newsflash.**

Create a headline/newsflash to summarise your learning. When asking for feedback, get students responding in different styles, e.g. in the style of a football commentator/children's TV presenter, etc.

- **Coming Soon to a Cinema Near You…**

Ask students to think of a film title/plot/slogan to summarise their learning/skills they have used and pitch it as a new film.

- **Explain Your Statement.**

Number students and number statements on the board. Have students explain their statements to the rest of their group as best they can. Give an opportunity for other students to intervene and add points if appropriate.

- **Which Picture?**

Place a variety of images on the board and ask students to relate their learning to one of the images, explaining why.

- **A-Z.**

As a challenge, ask students to write a word for each letter of the alphabet based on the skills they have used, something they have learnt or a keyword from the lesson.

- **Plot Your Learning.**

    Plot the steps of your learning on a timeline. What did you learn/when?

- **I Resign!**

    Swap roles with the students and ask them to teach you/the class about the topic. Ask questions like those that they would to extend their thinking and explaining skills.

- **Ready, Steady, Make as Many.**

    Place key words on the board and ask students to make as many phrases from them as they can.

- **Anagrams.**

    Provide anagrams of key words seen in the lesson, on the board or, have students creating their own and testing their partner.

- **Rate the Word.**

    Ask students to rate words based on a scale given or RAG them based on their understanding of them.

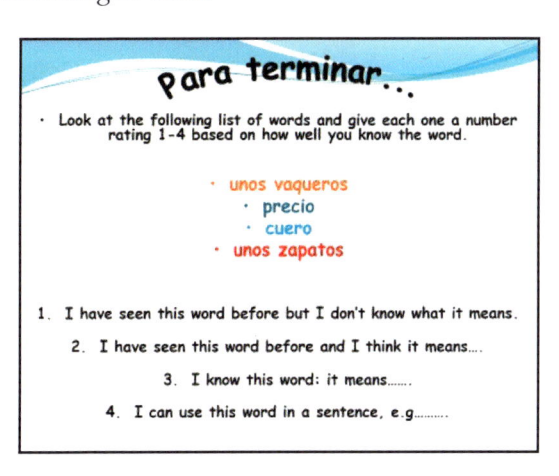

---

**Para terminar...**

- Look at the following list of words and give each one a number rating 1-4 based on how well you know the word.

    - unos vaqueros
    - precio
    - cuero
    - unos zapatos

1. I have seen this word before but I don't know what it means.
2. I have seen this word before and I think it means....
3. I know this word: it means.......
4. I can use this word in a sentence, e.g..........

Class dismissed!

# DEDICATION

I dedicate this book to my parents, Lloyd and Carrole Sargent, my fiancé Charlie Nundy and my form group, even though it is probably not "sick" to do so!

Mum and Dad, you will never truly understand how grateful I am to you both for always believing in me and supporting me in every way. You said you always knew I would be a teacher and as always, you were right. Your reassurance led me to do something that I love. It has not always been easy but then again, in the words of Dad: "If everything was easy, everyone would be doing it!" You have been there through the tantrums, tears and nerves in the run up to an observation, you have been pretend students when I have needed to trial a strategy and you have always provided great words of wisdom even if I acted as if I did not want to hear them at the time. It is a real honour to call you my parents, and although everyone says they have the best parents in the world, it cannot be true because I really do. John and I are so lucky to have you and even though I am your favourite, I guess I should thank my little bro too. Even though he is half way across the world, he always there with words of encouragement through the powers of WhatsApp and FaceTime!

You are both true inspirations to me and all that I have accomplished is down to the love, encouragement and sacrifices made by you guys and although it's impossible to thank you adequately for everything you've done, I hope I can continue to make you proud.

Charlie, we never really do the "lovey-dovey" thing, but I would just like you to know that without you by my side, none of this would be possible. You encouraged me to change careers in order to go into teaching and supported me wholeheartedly with all elements of it. In fact, without your praise and backing, this book would still just be a document saved on my laptop.

You may not believe in many things, but you have always believed in me and when things have been stressful, you have always been there to pick up the pieces. Most of the time it's through making awful jokes, the ones where I try really hard not to laugh but you make it impossible not to but it's also through you just simply being you. Your calming influence and laid-back attitude settles me and as much as I hate to admit it, your advice is normally right. I know I do not always show it but I am grateful for this advice and everything else you do, especially the sacrifices you make such as when you suggest putting the football on so I don't get distracted from my work. You are a real hero!

Finally, I dedicate this to my form who are currently in Year 10. You truly are an amazing bunch of young people who never fail to make me laugh on a daily basis. To me, you guys are what teaching is all about. Watching you grow from Year 7 to now has been a real privilege and in individual ways, from attaining great grades to winning sporting matches to raising money for charity, you make me so proud.

Just as I am supposed to teach you, you teach and inspire me and without a doubt, each one of you has a bright future ahead of you. Work hard and enjoy your school days but please stop eating share packs of crisps and pot noodles at 8:35 in the morning!

I am always going on at you about reading, but if you are going to read anything, make it this book! Who knows, maybe it could inspire you to go into the world of teaching one day and you too could be having a debate on what constitutes proper school shoes or uniform.

Make wise choices, listen to advice and always believe in yourself just as I believe in you all.

**Amy.**